Diary: How to Improve the World (You Will Only Make Matters Worse)

John Cage

Expanded Edition

Edited by Joe Biel and Richard Kraft
With an afterword by David W. Rose

siglio NEW YORK 2019

The editors and publisher wish to thank Laura Kuhn, director of the John Cage Trust, Emy Martin of the John Cage Trust, Suzanna Tamminen of Wesleyan University Press, and James Hoff of Primary Information.

Book and cover design: Natalie Kraft

Second printing paperback edition
ISBN: 978-1-938221-21-7
Printed and bound in China.

siglio uncommon books at the intersection of art & literature
PO BOX 234, South Egremont, MA 01258 Tel: 310-857-6935
www.sigliopress.com

Available to the trade through D.A.P./Artbook.com
75 Broad Street, Suite 630, New York, NY 10004
Tel: 212-627-1999 Fax: 212-627-9484

Part I

Diary: How to Improve the World
(You Will Only Make Matters Worse) 1965

6

Part II

Diary: How to Improve the World
(You *Will Only Make Matters Worse)*
Continued 1966

26

Part III

Diary: How to Improve the World
(You Will Only Make Matters Worse)
Continued 1967

46

Part IV

Diary: How to Improve the World
(You Will Only Make Matters Worse)
Continued 1968 (Revised)

67

Part V

Diary: How to Improve the World
(You Will Only Make Matters Worse)
Continued 1969 (Part V)

85

Part VI

Diary: How to Improve the World
(You Will Only Make Matters Worse)
Continued 1970–71

107

Part VII

Diary: How to Improve the World
(You Will Only Make Matters Worse)
Continued 1971–72

127

Part VIII

Diary: How to Improve the World
(You Will Only Make Matters Worse)
Continued 1973–1982

146

Editors' Note by Richard Kraft and Joe Biel

165

The Eleventh Thunderclap by David Rose

172

A selection of pages from the
incomplete and unpublished Part IX

176

This text was written for publication by Clark Coolidge in his magazine Joglars, *Providence, R.I. (Vol. 1, No. 3, 1966). It is a mosaic of ideas, statements, words, and stories. It is also a diary. For each day, I determined by chance operations how many parts of the mosaic I would write and how many words there would be in each. The number of words per day was to equal, or, by the last statement written, to exceed one hundred words.*

Since Coolidge's magazine was printed by photo-offset from typescripts, I used an IBM Selectric typewriter to print my text. I used twelve different type faces, letting chance operations determine which face would be used for which statement. So, too, the left marginations were determined, the right marginations being the result of not hyphenating words and at the same time keeping the number of characters per line forty-three or less. The present typography follows the original chance-determined plan.

I have several times given this text as a lecture, first at Beloit College in Wisconsin, more recently (June 1966) at the International Design Conference in Aspen, Colorado. It was thereafter reprinted in the spring 1967 issue of Aspen Magazine.

Diary: How to Improve the World (You Will Only Make Matters Worse) 1965

I. Continue; I'll discover where you sweat (Kierkegaard). We are getting rid of ownership, substituting use. Beginning with ideas. Which ones can we take? Which ones can we give? **Disappearance of power politics.** Non-measurement. *Japanese, he said : we also hear with our feet. I'd quoted Busoni : Standing between musician and music is notation. Before I'd given the history : chance operations, indeterminacy. I'd cited the musics of India : notation of them's after the fact. I'd spoken of direct musical action (since it's ears, not interposing eyes).* **2:00 A.M., Jensen said, "Even if you didn't like the results (Lindsay, etc.), we hope you liked the telling of it." Telling (?) of it! We were there while it was happening!** II. Minimum ethic : Do what you said you'd do. Impossible? Telephone. No answer? My idea was that if they wanted to fight (human nature and all that), they should do it in the Antarctic, rest of us gambling on daily outcome : proceeds for world welfare. Instead they're cooperative down there, exchanging data, being friendly. April '64 : U.S. State Department man gave Honolulu talk—"global village whether we like it or not"—, cited fifty-five services which are global in extent. Mountain range dividing Oahu, formerly crenelated (crenelations for self-

protection while shooting arrows),
is now tunneled, permitting population
circulation. Wars etc. part of dying
political-economic structures. Social
work equals **increasing number of**
global services. III. As McLuhan says,
everything happens at once. Image is
no longer stream falling over rocks,
getting from original to final place;
it's as Tenney explained : a vibrating
complex, any addition or subtraction
of component(s), regardless of apparent
position(s) in the total system,
producing alteration, a different music.
Fuller : As long as one human being is
hungry, the entire human race is
hungry. *City planning's obsolete. What's*
needed is global planning so Earth
may stop stepping like octopus on its
own feet. Buckminster Fuller uses his
head : comprehensive design science;
inventory of world resources. Conversion :
the mind turns around, no longer
facing in its direction. Utopia?
Self-knowledge. Some will make it,
with or without LSD. The others? Pray
for acts of God, crises, power
failures, no water to drink. IV. We
see symmetrically : canoe on northern
Canadian lake, stars in midnight sky
repeated in water, forested shores
precisely mirrored. Our hearing's
asymmetrical : noticed sounds surprise us,
echoes of shouts we make transform our
voices, straight line of sound from us to

shore's followed by echo's slithering
around the lake's perimeter. *When I said, "Fifty-five global services," California Bell Telephone man replied (September '65), "It's now sixty-one."*
The seasons (creation, preservation, destruction, quiescence) : this was experience and resultant idea (no longer is : he flies to Rio). What shall we wear as we travel about? A summer suit with or without long underwear? What about Stein's idea : People are the way their land and air is? V. When I said that culture was changing from Renaissance to what it is now (McLuhan), Johns objected to what he said was an oversimplification. But Johns was speaking according to our non-Renaissance experience : total field, non-focused multiplicity. *We are, are we not, socially speaking, in a situation of the old dying and the new coming into being? For the old—paying bills, seeking for power—take the attitude of play : games. For the new—doing what isn't necessary, "moving sand from one part of the beach to another" (Buckminster Fuller)—take the religious attitude : cerebration. (It celebrates.) The people have left. The cat and kittens were taken to the SPCA. The house is full of fleas.* VI. They say totally determined music and indeterminate music sound the same. I visited Hamada. Getting up from

the wheel, he said, "I'm not interested
in results; just going on. *Art's in*
process of coming into its own : life.
The lake is undefined. The land around
rests upon it obscuring its shape, shape
that needs to remain unrevealed. Sung.
"Floating world." Rain, curtain of wind-
swept lake's surface beyond : second view
(there are others, he tells me, one with
mists rising). Yesterday it was stillness
and reflections, groups of bubbles. An
American garden : water, not sand,
vegetation, not stones. Thunder.
Without intending to, I'm going from lake
to lake. Saltair. Salt Lake. *VII.*
Hugh Nibley. I hadn't seen him since
high school days. I asked him what
he thought about other planets and
sentient populations. Yes, he said,
throughout the universe : it's Mormon
doctrine. We'd said good-bye. I opened
the door of the car, picked up my
attaché case and everything in it fell
out on the grass and the gutter. His
comment : Something memorable always
happens. Things we were going to do are
now being done by others. They were, it
seems, not in our minds to do (were we
or they out of our minds?) but simply
ready to enter any open mind, any mind
disturbed enough not to have an idea in
it. VIII. The daily warmth we
experience, my father said, is not
transmitted by Sun to Earth, but is what
Earth does in response to Sun.

Measurements, he said, measure measuring means. *Bashō : Matsutake ya shiranu ko no ha no hebaritsuku. The leaf of some unknown tree sticking on the mushroom (Blythe). Mushroom does not know that leaf is sticking on it (Takemitsu). Project : Discover way to translate Far Eastern texts so western men can read orientally. Communication? Bakarashi! Words without syntax, each word polymorphic.* He wanted me to agree that the piano tuner and the piano maker have nothing to do with it (the composition). The younger ones had said : Whoever makes the stretcher isn't separate from the painting. (It doesn't stop there either.) *IX. Looking in all directions not just one direction.* Housing (Fuller) will be, like telephoning, a service. Only circumstance to stop your living there : someone's there already (it's busy). Thus we'll learn to desire emptiness. Not being able to say, "This is mine," we'll want when we inquire to get no response at all. **4:00 P.M. throughout the world. Whether we like it or not (is what he said) it's happening to us.** Advertisements are all good; the news is all bad (McLuhan). But how we receive bad news can change : we're glad to hear unemployment's increasing. Soon, all that will be required of us will be one hour's work per year (Fuller). **X. They ask what**

the purpose of art is. Is that how things are? Say there were a thousand artists and one purpose, would one artist be having it and all the nine hundred and ninety-nine others be missing the point? Arcata Bottom sign said : Experiment endlessly and keep humble. "Write to the Center for the Study of Democratic Institutions; they'll know about the global services." I did. They answered they knew nothing, suggested writing to State Department. Books one formerly needed were hard to locate. Now they're all out in paperback. Society's changing. Relevant information's hard to come by. Soon it'll be everywhere, unnoticed.

XI. Electronics. *Day comes, the day we die.* There's less and less to do : circumstances do it for us. Earth. Old reasons for doing things no longer exist. (Sleep whenever. Your work goes on being done. You and it no longer have a means of separation.) We had the chance to do it individually. Now we must do it together : globally. War will not be group conflict : it'll be murder, pure and simple, individually conceived. Curiosity, awareness. They returned to the fact that we all need to eat to explain their devotion to money rather than music. When I spoke of the equation, work equals money equals virtue, they interrupted me (they didn't let me say

that nowadays there's no equation),
saying, "How can you speak of money and
virtue in the same breath?" XII. Where
there doesn't seem to be any space,
know we no longer know what space is.
Have faith space is there, giving one
the chance to renovate his way of
recognizing it, no matter the means,
psychic, somatic, or means
involving extensions of either.
People still ask for definitions, but
it's quite clear now that nothing
can be defined. Let alone art, its
purpose etc. We're not even sure of
carrots (whether they're what we think
they are, how poisonous they are, who
grew them and under what circumstances).
She was indignant when I suggested
the use of an aphrodisiac. Why?
Naturally she considers TV a waste of
time. **XIII. The purpose of one**
activity is no longer separate from the
purpose of any other activity. All
activities fuse in one purpose which
is (cf. Huang-Po Doctrine of Universal
Mind) no purpose. Imitate the
Ganges' sands, becoming indifferent to
perfume, indifferent to filth.
Influence. Where does it come from?
Responsibility? Sick ones now are
heartsick. Narcissi, they became
entranced with emotions, purposes,
mystified by living in the twentieth
century. We've invented something else,
not the wheel. We extended nervous

systems. McLuhan : ***Agenbite of Outwit***
(Location, Spring '63). (The inability of
people to be inactive. As Satie said :
If I don't smoke, someone else will in
my place. Audience participation,
active passivity.) XIV. Since the
Spirit's omnipresent, there's a difference
in things but no difference in spirit.
McLuhan was able to say "The medium is
the message" because he started from
no concern with content. Or choose
quantity, not quality (we get
quality willy-nilly) : i.e. we'd like
to stay alive, the changes that are
taking place are so many and so
interesting. Composition'll have, he
said, less and less to do with what
happens. Things happen more
quickly. One of the signs you'll get
that'll tell you things are going well is
that you and everyone else you know will
be inhabiting lightweight Dymaxion
houses, disengaged from ownership and
from violated Earth spot (read
Fuller). **XV. Smiling, she said, let**
the old ones walk out : there's not
much to be done about them in any case.
Distractions? Interruptions? Welcome
them. They give you the chance to
know whether you're disciplined. That
way you needn't bother about sitting
cross-legged in the lotus position.
Phonetics. **He was a physicist and a**
computer-composer in his spare time.
Why was he so stupid? Because he was

of the opinion that the only thing that will engage the intellect is the measurement of relations between things? When told that his mind could change, his response was, "How? Why?" Conflict won't be between people and people but between people and things. In this conflict let's try to arrange matters so the outcome as in philosophy will never be decisive. Treat redwoods, for instance, as entities that have at least a chance to win. XVI. He wanders through markets as though they were forests and he an exploring botanist (throws nothing away). Lake. *Take what you're working on with you, if, that is, you have something to* do. *Gaps.* What a pity that she should feel obliged to take matters into her own hands! (There's practically no kitchen, he says, and it's already been figured out that money's being saved.) *Mexico.* Europeans are still up against it. They seem to require a center of interest. They understand tragedy but life itself (and any art that's like it) puzzles them, seems unsatisfactory. We're starved for entertainment (thanking the two women). XVII. By becoming angry I simply altered my biochemistry, bringing about a two-hour recovery. Meanwhile circumstances continued characterized by habit. Going in different directions we get instead of

separation **a sense of space.** *Music as*
discourse (jazz) doesn't work. *If*
you're going to have a discussion,
have it and use words. *(Dialogue is*
another matter.) **Acts and facts.**
Straw that breaks the camel's back :
their saying No (they advertise they'll
say Yes). *Principles?* *Then all's*
intolerable. *No principles (which*
doesn't mean we fail to become
furious). *So?* *We swim, drowning now*
and then. **I must write and tell him**
about beauty, the urgency to avoid
it. **XVIII.** **Hearing of past actions**
(politics, economics), people soon
won't be able to imagine how such
things could've happened. **Fusing**
politics with economics prepared
disappearance of both. **Still**
invisible. *Arriving, realizing we*
never departed. He mentioned heads
on the ceiling. Seeing them, noticed
him too. Fusion of credit card with
passport. Means of making one's voice
heard : refusal to honor credit card.
End of the month? That too may be
changed : the measurement of time,
what season it is, whether it's
night or day. In any case, no bills,
just added information. *"Take it easy,*
but take it." What'll we do? (Before
lunch.) "Wing it." XIX. Wanting list of
current global services, how'll I get
it? Long costly correspondences?
(Pentagon advises telephoning.) I'll

write to the President (of the U.S.), to
the Secretary (of State of the U.S.).
Time passing, I'll ask those I
encounter whether they've any
information. (McLuhan hadn't any.)
I'll write to Fuller. Should have done
that in the first place (Pope Paul,
Lindsay : Take note). *Amateur (used to
say, "Don't touch it!") now speaks of
audience participation, feels something,
anything, is needed, would help. Develop
panopticity of mind (Listen).* What'll
happen when intelligence is recognized
as a global resource (Fuller)?
Political organizations—giving up
involvement with play (partners,
opponents), involvement with unattainable
goals (victories, truths,
freedoms)—will simply fade out of the
picture. Image coming up is that of
the utilities (gas, electricity,
telephones) : unquestionable, emotionally
unarousing. XX. What is a drawing?
No one knows any longer. Something
that doesn't require that you wait
while you're making it for it to dry?
Something on paper? Museum director
said (Tobey, Schwitters), "It's a
question of emphasis." **Thanksgiving.
Art. Transportation plan (eventually at no
monetary cost, conveyances recognized
for what they are : extensions of each human
being and his luggage) : short distances
costly (to taxi for one block is a
luxury), long trips cheap as dirt**

(crossing continents, oceans). Effect of videophone on travel? That we'll stay home, settling like gods for impressions we'll give of being everywhere at once? XXI. Everywhere where economics and politics obtain (everywhere?), policy is dog eat dog. Take taxi tolls between cities. Those in one town higher than those in the other. Driver going from one to the other must drive home alone. Relaxation of rules, ties (Take marriage), is indicated. *Now that we've got the four-lane roads, we won't have any use for them. (Good for roller-skating, he said.)* Refuse value judgments. Since time lags were inordinately long, change's now welcome. Advertising's discredited itself. When they advertise something, we avoid it. There's nothing we really need to do that isn't dangerous. Eighth Street artists knew this years ago : constantly spoke of risk. But what's meant by risk? Lose something? Property, life? Principles? The way to lose our principles is to examine them, to give them an airing. XXII. Heaven's no longer paved with gold (changes in church architecture). Heaven's a motel. She changed part of the loft : wall-to-wall carpeting, mobile TV. No conflicts. Twenty-two telephone calls were made by Betty Zeiger "disrupting efficiency of federal agencies . . . dedicated to pursuit of peace." STATE DEPARTMENT SAID HAWAII SPEAKER WAS A WOMAN. FIFTY-FIVE (NOW SIXTY-ONE) GLOBAL SERVICES ARE IN AREA OF HUMANITIES "BEYOND MERE PROVISION OF FOOD/SHELTER." NOT TECHNOLOGICAL SERVICES. State Department : Global village developed from "Literary Villages" (plan for the betterment of life in India). **"We are packages of leaking water." "The next water you drink may be your** own."

XXIII. **Let's call it the collective consciousness (we've got the collective unconscious). The question is : what are the things everyone needs regardless of likes and dislikes? Beginning of answer : Water, food, shelter, clothing, electricity, audio-visual communication, transportation. Form of answer : Global utilities network.** Do not fear that as the globe gets utility organized your daily life will not remain (or become as the case may be) disorganized, characterized by chaos, illuminated anarchically. You'll have nothing to do; so what will you do? A lifelong university (Fuller)? **In the lobby after La Monte Young's music stopped, Geldzahler said : It's like being in a womb; now that I'm out, I want to get back in. I felt differently and so did Jasper Johns : We were relieved to be released.** XXIV. Knowing-seeing,

conforming with reality. Anscombe's
a feminist, insists on wearing pants.
Obliged to lecture dressed in a
dress, she took one with her,
changed into it, lectured, changed back,
walked home (teaching all the time) in
pants. As was said, "When will you
undress yourself of your ideas?" No
escape. Billy Klüver said decision
of judge in South America (e.g.) is
taken as precedent by judge in Sweden.
Brown's work (Life Against Death) *is*
prophetic (also de Kooning's remark : we no
longer have tragedy; the situation an
individual may be in is only pathetic) :
society as a mass is what needs
psychoanalysis. (Thus polymorphous
perversity, necessity of Utopia.) Looking
at billions, unlike Nehru, we must
treat them as one person. **XXV. She**
says life is like a blank wall,
impassible. Correct deduction : she is
in love. Klüver : ITU lists many
international agreements re Morse code,
telegrams, telephones, radio, television,
emergency signals, meteorological
information, frequencies and powers
of stations, means to prevent
static. "How would it be if these
agreements didn't exist?" (ITU asks.)
"No press-news, no pictures in the
papers, no exchanged radio programs, no
static-free radio reception, no
meteorological prognoses, no storm
warnings, no security at sea, in air."

Klüver reports : ITU (International Telecommunication Union) was established in 1865 (nine years older than UPU—post—and seventeen older than railroad agreements). *XXVI. The truth is that everything causes everything else. We do not speak therefore of one thing causing another.* There are no secrets. It's just we thought they said dead when they said bread. Or that we weren't tuned in when transmission took place. **Being told about global services, Barnett Newman emphasized the importance of the arts. Society has tape recorders, radio broadcasts, and also copyright laws (which it considers extending). (Gets in its own way.) Get rid of copyright (this text is copyright). We're making nonspecialist interpenetrations.** *Automation.* **Alteration of global society through electronics so that world will go round by means of united intelligence rather than by means of divisive intelligence (politics, economics). Say this idea has no basis in fact but arose through brushing of misinformation. No sweat. It arose (the idea exists, is fact).** XXVII. Do not imagine there aren't many things to do. We need for instance an utterly wireless technology. Just as Fuller domes (dome within dome, translucent, plants between) will give

impression of living in no home at
all (outdoors), so all technology
must move toward way things were
before man began changing them :
identification with nature in her manner
of operation, complete mystery. Fuller
prophecy at end of Tomkins profile
of him editorially (*New Yorker*)
eliminated. Subject : global
network for electrical power (including
China who'd participate in a spirit
of practicality). Fuller's remarks
considered laughable in view of
November blackout. (We need another
blackout, one that isn't so pleasant,
one that'll suggest using our heads the
way Fuller used his.) *XXVIII. We've*
poisoned our food, polluted our air
and water, killed birds and cattle,
eliminated forests, impoverished,
eroded the earth. We're unselfish,
skillful : we include in our acts to
perform—we've had a rehearsal—
the last one. What would you call it?
Nirvana? **"Not only was instant**
universal voice communication forecast
by David Sarnoff, but also instant
television, instant newspapers, instant
magazines and instant visual
telephone service . . . the development of
such global communications system
would link people everywhere . . . for
reorientation toward a 'one-world
concept of mass communications in an
era marked by the emergence of a

universal language, a universal culture and a universal common market.'" *XXIX. Population. Art's obscured the difference between art and life. Now let life obscure the difference between life and art. Fuller's life is art : comprehensive design science, inventory of world resources (if enough mined copper exists, re-use it, don't mine more : same with ideas). World needs arranging. It'll be like living a painting by Johns :* Stars and Stripes*'ll be utilities, our daily lives the brushstrokes. McLuhan : Work's obsolete. Why? Work's partial involvement in activity. Activity is now necessarily total involvement (cf. work of artists, work not involved in profit). Why total involvement? Electronics. Why everything-at-once? The way we-things are. Yathabhutam.* **Where there's a history of organization (art), introduce disorder. Where there's a history of disorganization (world society), introduce order. These directives are no more opposed to one another than mountain's opposed to spring weather. "How can you believe this when you believe that?" How can I not? Long life.**

Once one gets interested in world improvement, there is no stopping. I began the following text immediately after finishing the first one. I gave it a length approximately the same but slightly different. The notebooks in which I wrote it were with me wherever I went. I finished it early in September 1966 in Pontpoint (par Pont-Sainte-Maxence) north of Paris in the country home of John de Menil and in the room where Montesquieu, I was told, had also written and on a not too dissimilar subject. It was accepted by Maxine Groffsky for publication in the Spring 1967 issue of the Paris Review.

Diary: How to Improve the World
(You *Will Only Make Matters Worse)*
Continued 1966

XXX. The most, the best, we can do, we
believe (wanting to give evidence of
love), is to get out of the way, leave
space around whomever or whatever it is.
But there is no space! Difference between
pennilessness now and pennilessness then :
now we've got unquestioned credit. *"In
the Beginning was the Word." Pulpul Jayakar
(straight from India), talking about
computers, said : An explosion of the Word;
communication without language! (We'll
still speak : a) for practical reasons; b)
for the pleasure of it; c) to say what
should/shouldn't be done.)* Bird up and
overhead. Friends we no longer see.
Gone. Some died. *XXXI. Mexico, India
Canada (changing citizenship).* **Electronic
democracy (instantaneous voting on the
part of anyone) : no sheep. World
credit.** Hearing my thoughts, he asked : ARE
YOU A MARXIST? ANSWER : I'M AN
ANARCHIST, same as you are when you're
telephoning, turning on/off the lights,
drinking water. Private prospect of
enlightenment's no longer sufficient. Not
just self- but social-realization. Fuller
spoke of Semantography, universal picture
language devised by C.K. Bliss, said
it was rich in nouns while what we
need's verbs. *Servant problem.* What's
what? (Russia, U.S.A.) Which is which? I
mentioned drugs. Kremen said the human
mind's interesting enough in the
non-toxic state. XXXII. Asked about
housing utility, Fuller pointed out

electrically-lit roadside telephone booths, twenty-four hour use of facilities. (How this came about escaped our notice, no voting or purchase involved. Bed, food, bath to be expected, added to telephone or available elsewhere : decentralization of living.) Up by our bootstraps! Lost in two different ways. There was also a fire to put out. **Alone (no one to disagree with).** **Chess.** **Asked what he did, he said he'd studied meteorology, passed examinations, graduated, that weather's simple to predict. (What had his teachers had in mind?) "There's no reason for the mistakes that are generally** made."

XXXIII. Changes in aquariums : all the fish in the same tank; no Latin information. Cross-Texas, eighty miles per hour, radio rocks and rolls (now I listen) : "If it's a game, I won't play it. Don't just stand there. Tell me what's, what's, what's, what's on your mind." He registered as a conscientious objector. Drafted anyway, he was put on a train going south. He escaped, was caught, spent a year in service. Then, since he never cashed any of the checks they'd given him, he received an honorable discharge. (Russian chickens had diseased muscles. Chemical therapies failed. Suddenly, The chickens were healthy. The *muscular tissues'd been reduced to chaos, disorganized by electrical means.)*

XXXIV. Bodhisattva Doctrine : Enter
Nirvana only when all beings, sentient,
non-sentient, are ready to do likewise.
Couldn't believe my eyes (stopping for
lunch in Red Bud, Illinois) : a single
photograph of nature (mountains,
lake, island, forests) enlarged, printed
twice, once left to right, once right to
left, the two prints juxtaposed to form a
single image, seam down the middle.
Eugenics. Proposal : take facts of
art seriously : try them in economics/
politics, giving up, that is, notions about
balance (of power, of wealth),
foreground, background. They will kill
you, she said, with kindness. There's a
temptation to do nothing simply because
there's so much to do that one doesn't
know where to begin. Begin anywhere. For
instance, since electronics is at
the heart of the matter, establish a
global voltage, a single design for
plugs and jacks. Remove the need for
transformers and adaptors. Vary not the
connecting means but the things to be
connected. XXXV. Way's being found to
overcome problem inherent in painting and
sculpture (fact of object) : laser
projection of three-dimensional images.
To remove object place your hand in thin
air behind it. What's interesting about
minds is they work differently.
What's interesting about one mind is that
it works in different ways. Hunting for
one thing, finding another. Gardens

that seem uncultivated : Tinguely's at
Soissy-sur-École. *I remember clams from the
Sound exhibited years ago in a Seattle
aquarium (near the Farmer's Market,
admission ten cents) : their movement,
their timing of it. They were a bed,
immobile, one on top of the other,
two feet deep in a tank of water, sand
on the bottom of the tank. We were told
to wait.* **XXXVI.** Weather feels good.
Isn't. More rain is needed. Water.
He played two games, winning one, losing
the other. He was continually himself,
totally involved in each game, unmoved
by the outcome of either. What's the
nature of his teaching? For one
thing : devotion (practice gives evidence
of it). For another : not just
playing half the game but playing all of
it (having a view that includes that of
the opponent). Suddenly a clam rose to
the surface directly, remained there a
moment, then descended slowly,
leaf-like, tipping one way, then the
other, arriving at the bottom to produce
a disturbance, such that clam after clam
did likewise, sometimes several, sometimes
many, sometimes not one at all,
producing a dance that completely
involved us. (Doing all that we *needed to*
do). **XXXVII. Projects involving many
people and many interruptions go well.
Private concerns stumble along.** The
fact that their parents have separated doesn't
disturb the children. They go on

looking at television. How old should they be before they smoke marijuana? No one seems to know. Tolstoy : art properly arouses religious emotion (conduces to brotherhood all mankind, no *boundaries).* Skinner : "Let us agree to start with, that health is better than illness, wisdom better than ignorance, love better than hate, and productive energy *better than neurotic* sloth. **We invented machines in order to reduce our work. Now that we have them we think we should go on working (Committee of eight on Automation, Economics and Employment considering whether U.S. society should be geared for employment or unemployment voted six to two in favor of employment).** XXXVIII. *"I* **breathe."** Starvation. THERE'S NO STOPPING. The garden's a bungalow. The sky's its roof. Hedges form the rectangular rooms. Apple tree, admired, split as though struck by lightning. Coincidence? Branch of it's on the lawn like a picture that's not hanging straight. Flowers **are withering. Gardener's on vacation.** Mud is on the windshield, fallen branches wherever we go. *Sky's ready for launching of missiles. "He hit me first."* We're open-minded. Result : idea leaving head that had it returns transformed. Individual's thoughts become social projects. "World's O.K. as is" : "Work to make the world O.K." Moksha transformed is artha from which it was a

liberation. Spirit's materialized
Kama? Walking along, it'll happen we touch
one another, falling immediately in love.
XXXIX. If a Utopia such as Skinner '48
described (*Walden Two*), doesn't
exist, why doesn't it? If it does,
what aren't we all in it? What traitor
thinks makes clear what nation's mind's
become. Pound's refrain : down with
usury. Lincoln : Unless next President
outlaws private banking, America in
hundred years'll be in worse situation
than it (Civil War) is. **Rest of the
world's suffered surgery so it won't be
India. Indian standing by New Jersey
waterfall seeing the surface of the pool
below white with the suds of detergents,
jammed with beer cans, suggested
containers that one could eat. Different
flavors. Things that return to
nature.** XL. To finance Union vs.
Confederacy, Lincoln authorized
private banking in the U.S.A. Credit
(conventionally 9/10ths of economic
power, actual money constituting the
remaining tenth) became the property
of bankers. The notion is that not
everyone'll want his deposit back at the
same time. Nine times as much as a banker
had was safely to be loaned for interest.
As the story goes : Dad ran away, came
to a ranch, was given a job irrigating (a
job that'd kept several men busy every
day all day long). He looked the land
over, made something, dug something (can't

remember which). No further work was necessary. Seeing he had nothing to do, they fired him. XLI. WE'RE GETTING RID OF THE HABIT WE HAD OF EXPLAINING EVERYTHING. **Margaret Mead's idea re metropolitan transportation (Duchamp had same idea in 'twenties) : private cars parked at city limits; city cars used as one uses carts in super-markets and airports, abandoned at one's destination. Police busy returning cars to parking lots, getting them serviced or repaired whenever necessary.** Basic Economic Security (Robert Theobald : *Free Men and Free Markets*) : everyone'll have what he needs. Wanting things that are scarce, he'll make them, find them, get them (as long as supply lasts) in return for having done something machines don't do. **The mushrooms appeared sooner even than I expected.** XLII. To know whether or not art is contemporary, we no longer use aesthetic criteria (if it's destroyed by shadows, spoiled by ambient sounds); (assuming these) we use social **criteria : can include action on the part of others. We'll take the mad ones with us, and we know where we're going. Even now, he told me, they sit at the crossroads in African villages regenerating society. Mental hospitals : localization of a resource we've yet to exploit.** I VISITED AN AGING ANARCHIST. (HE HAD THE REMAINING COPIES OF MARTIN'S *MEN AGAINST THE STATE*.) HE

INTRODUCED ME TO TWO NEGRO **children he'd adopted. After they went out to play he told me what trouble he'd had in deciding finally to draw this line : No jumping up and down on the beds.** **XLIII. As he travels from one place to another, he leaves things** *behind. He needs help but no one knows where he is.* DON'T KNOW WHAT to read, *Love's Body* or *out-of-date newspapers that are lying around. Everything we come across is to the point.* **Living underground because there was no money. Arizona land and air permitted making mounds, covering them with cement, excavating to produce rooms, providing these with skylights. For anyone approaching, the community was invisible. Cacti, desert plants : the land seemed undisturbed. Quantity (abundance) changes what's vice, what's virtue. Selfishness is out; carelessness is in. (Waste's characteristic.) "Don't be a litterbug." "Keep North Carolina** *green." Scratch* the Ten Commandments. One of the new *ones : Thou Shalt Not Live (in addition to birth control, control of birth, euthanasia). What nature did we now must do.* XLIV. Bad politics (Souvtchinsky) produce good art. But of what use is good art? (Johns said he could imagine a world without it and that there was no reason to think it would not be a better one.) *He had been trained as a singer. Gave up music for* *cooking. Started a small restaurant, busy three times a day instead of theatrically once (even then not everyday).* **Julian Beinart said that, when being chauffeured in South Africa, he noticed Negro hitchhikers, tribesmen who cover their bodies with a fly-attracting grease, flies being considered the finest ornament, he asked the chauffeur to pick the people up, the chauffeur refused. Chauffeur said the grease left in the car would be nearly impossible to remove : "You'd never get rid of the flies."**

XLV. A meal **without mushrooms is like a day without rain.** Raised as a Methodist, I've never taken drugs. When a physicist told me electrodes near my ears would remove my sense of balance or, were I flying through space and the capsule was revolving, make me think my balance was normal, I was fascinated. Asking Duchamp why I accept electronics, refusing chemistry, he said, "It's not against the law." **George Herbert Mead's discussion of the religious attitude : first one thinks of himself as one of a family, later as part of a community, then as living in a city, citizen of such and such a country; finally, he feels no limit to that of which he is a part.**

XLVI. The past? Fuller's answer : Keep it. Times Square, for instance : cover it with a dome; put in tables, chairs, plastic carpeting. (Keep what remains so it's there to be enjoyed, not just read

about.) Chinese proceed differently, Häger reports. Revolting against themselves, they send tradition-maintaining artists, actors, musicians off to hard labor in distant places. Clean slate. After each war, industry offers new products for sale. The benefits from the present conflicts (hot and cold, on earth, in space) will be enormous. No organization, school, for instance, will be able to afford them. The only customer (not just rich but big enough to use them) will be the globe itself. XLVII. All the garbage cans in West Germany are the same size. They have lids designed so that the only thing one has to do is place them at the back of the garbage truck. The truck does the rest : picks them up, turns them upside-down, opens the lid, receives the garbage, closes the lid, sets them back on the street right-side-up. After getting the information from a small French manual, I was glad to discover that *Lactarius piperatus* and *L. vellereus,* large white mushrooms growing plentifully wherever I hunt, are indeed excellent when grilled. Raw, these have a milk that burns the tongue and throat. Cooked, they're delicious. Indigestion. **XLVIII. How will one discipline himself?** *More than he needs of everything'll do* **it for him.** He told me one of the things he noticed among the people who were using marijuana and LSD

was that they didn't *bother with the*
conventions of greeting one another or
saying good-bye. **Open and closed**
communities (a botanical expression) :
disturbing the earth, men have opened
it up. Seeds and spores in the air
have a chance to land, to live. Laws
we need to break : law forbidding stops
along the highway except for emergencies
or at designated points; law prohibiting
the picking of useful plants. XLIX.
Home begins outside. Shelter's inside.
[Buckminster Fuller's *Profile of the*
Industrial Revolution. Technical
acquisition by science of ninety-two atomic
elements accomplished in 1932. Same year
(John McHale comments) gold as a
certificate of wealth was abandoned in
the U.S.A.] *Examine the papers, the*
books, to see what ideas were had that
could be, but weren't, put to use. Not
only ideas but inventions that worked :
Dad's dehydrator that worked
electrostatically, separating refuse
oil into dry chemicals, water that
could be drunk, oil of the highest grade,
his means for preventing lightning.
Picturephone : limited commercial service
now **provided between New York, Chicago, and**
Washington. Limitation : customers must
be highly involved in business,
government and/or war. L. Abundance.
Officials checked to make certain we'd
paid air-travel tax, didn't ask to see
our passports. Marcel Duchamp.

**". . . Valencia, cathedral—University.
Palma will be interesting again, then
Dardona and off to Milan and after which
the western coast of Yugoslavia & tour
(at southern end) of Grecian Islands
after which plane from Athens to New York.
Many travelers—going everywhere.
Love, Mom" More irritated by the
schedule than the work, he announced
he'd do all the dishwashing. Shortly the
others were helping. Sometimes he had
nothing to do.** Returning from
Europe : "We're all looking forward
to the return of the W.P.A. It's the
only thing we ever had any talent for."
LI. "Utopia for practical purposes."
*Tall Jewish teenager just ahead of me,
his mother, wanting to go shopping,
concerned whether he'd be able to file
his passport application without her
help. After several departures, always
coming back, she finally left the crowded*
**room. Discovering that he'd play chess, I
brought out my portable magnetic set.
Standing in line, we played two games,
leaving the second one unfinished.**
The cows in India, not understanding
traffic lights, cross intersections
whenever they reach them. Motorists
never get angry. They wait patiently. The
evening's air's heavy with the odor of
burning cow-dung, fuel used for cooking.
Buffalo enterprise : manufacture of
contraceptives for cows. Fewer cows :
more food for the starving millions.

LII. Story Agam told : "I'm looking for a key I lost over there." "Why not look, then, where you *lost it?*" *"It's* too dark over there. I look for it here where there's light." **Television up-to-date, things televised aren't. Receiving set, appliances up-to-date, home isn't. Architecture : "Environment control facility"**, "dwelling advantage" (Fuller), "each progressive model obsolete . . . materials scrapped, reprocessed", ("more with less") "instituting . . . world industry . . ." — "Include . . . design of . . . services, maintenance, parts inventories and transportation performances required to make . . . service operable around the world." (John McHale.) "Allowing any **kind of living." Weights, measures. Music having too many or not enough notes in it (Takahashi's preference). LIII. The father's a dope addict. The mother (two days ago—they came in white coats, white car, using flashlights, asking, "Where's the mad woman?") was taken away in a straitjacket. The children sleep at home, playing and having their meals next door. (Perpetual motion.) Removing social controls to points where they escape our notice. Examine situations. Make decisions. Implement them. [I asked Fuller whether he played chess. He said he used to, but that now he plays only one (the biggest) game. He does this energetically, globally ("I have a strong constitution"), encouraging** youth who've inherited from television, their "third parent," world consciousness. "They think 'world' . . . Theirs will be the most powerful and constructive revolution in all history."] LIV. More we leave the land, the more productive it becomes. Technique for changing society : education *followed by unemployment.* Article by Avner Hovne on automation (*Impact of Science on Society* 15:1, Unesco publication). Continuity values giving way to flexibility values. Automation alters what's done and where we do it. You could always tell when she was about to go out of her mind. She would begin to speak the truth. April '64 : fifty-five global services. September '65 : sixty-one global services. No one I speak to knows anything about them. I have no list, don't know what the number, August '66, is. Instead I read what I find in bookstores, libraries, getting clues here and there. World Health. World Food. Listened to Fuller on the 'phone, heard him insist : "World—not international—Man." LV. In connection with space travel, the Russians, they say, have found a means to induce sleep electronically. In twenty or thirty minutes one can get as much rest as eight or nine hours normally provide. Economics (money). Bernard Monnier said : Yes. "It's a question of credit, entirely fictional, conventional." Asked whether it's finally a matter of personalities (not masks but the feelings people give one another), he again said : Yes. "It's a question of *one person having confidence in another."* **Mobility, immobility. Artists never had enough time to do their work. Their lives always ended before the completion of their projects. Leisure, present or future, is not a social problem. Perhaps the fact we haven't gotten to know one another makes us think that people have nothing to do. LVI. Urgency.** EXPRESSION OF "LOSING TEMPO" IN CHESS. OBLIGATION TO RETREAT, TO MOVE A PIECE ONE'S MOVED, TO PROCEED IN A WAY HAVING NOTHING TO DO WITH ONE'S PLAN. TAKE TIME, HE SAYS. MOVE, BUT ONLY AFTER YOU'RE FULLY AWARE OF ALL THE POSSIBILITIES. X-QUANTITIES. *Indian philosophy and society at loggerheads : Indian society limited to family;* family's defined as stopping at the seventh relationship. Another error, Japanese : the refusal to be formally introduced (brings about philanthropies one doesn't want to **practice).** The property at Pontpoint. Formality and informality mixed : elegance without pretense (an unessential difference between the front and kitchen doors). One mistake : only the servants have TV. At table we converse. After coffee we play solitaire,

chess, now and then glancing at the
paintings and sculpture ("Everything's been
looked at"). Four P.M. we go
hunting for mushrooms. "Another part of
the forest." **LVII. Discussing her
travels, a lady mentioned she'd been
in Mallorca. When she was asked where
that was, she said she had no idea. "We
flew." (Sky's heavily clouded : grey
even black, some white. There are patches
of blue.)** Bureaucracy. He got the
notion his ideas belonged to him. He
refused to disclose them, fearing someone
else would profit from them. He made
contracts no one cared to sign. *The
view that all's equal (equal rights) is not
different from the view that all's
unequal (unique).* **No likes or dislikes
implicit in** either view.
**Non-obstruction. Criticism becomes
design (one's faculties used before
rather than after something's done).
Dialogue.** LVIII. (Music's made it
perfectly clear : we have all the time in
the world. What used timidly to take
eight minutes to play we now extend
to an hour. People thinking we're
not occupied converse with us while we're
performing.) Suzuki's lecture on Yu,
the principle **of not-knowing, a
not-knowing never to become a knowing.
Toward the end he laughed gently,
without expressing any accomplishment,** and
said, "Isn't it funny? I come all the
way from Japan to explain something to you

which of its nature is not to be explained?" Composer, who no longer arranges sounds in a piece, simply facilitates an enterprise. Using a telephone, he locates materials, services, raises money to pay for them. LIX. Mother wrote to say : "Stay in Europe. Soak up as much beauty as you possibly can." **Cards punched for insertion in telephones so we don't have to remember numbers or spend time dialing.** Acceleration. **What shall we do with our emotions? ("Suffer them," I hear her saying.)** Having everything we need, we'll nevertheless spend restless nights awake with desire for pleasures we *imagine that never take place. Things also happen gradually (one of New Babylon's anarchists was elected a member of Amsterdam's City Council). We've the right, Fuller explains, to object to slavery, segregation, etc. (the problem of work is solved : machines take the place of* muscles); we've not yet the right to object to war : first we must design, then implement means for making the world's resources the possession of all men. *LX. American anarchist, 1900, admitting failure, retired to the South of France. Dad's airplane engine, 1918, flew to pieces before it left the ground. Alloys needed to* contain the power were still undiscovered. Discover dialectics for ultra-high voltages (global electrical networks). Change society so differences are refreshing, nothing to do with possessions/power. *Octavio and Marie-José (we'll meet again in Mexico). Narayana Menon had said, "You'll like the Ambassador; he's a poet." I asked Paz whether being a diplomat took too much time from his poetry. He said* **it didn't. "There is no trade between the two countries. They are on the very best of relations."**

Now that the following text is written (it was published in the summer of 1967 by the Something Else Press, New York City, as a part of their Great Bear Pamphlet Series, using a color structure which followed a suggestion by Dick Higgins), I plan, circumstances permitting, to write further on the same subject. Just before Christmas I visited my mother who lives in a nursing home. (Two years ago she suffered a severe heart attack which left her physically helpless.) I told her I'd written three texts on world improvement. She said, "John! How dare *you? You should be ashamed!" Then she added, "I'm surprised at you." I asked her, in view of world conditions, whether she didn't think there was room for improvement. She said, "There certainly is. It makes good sense."*

Diary: How to Improve the World (You Will Only Make Matters Worse) Continued 1967

LXI. U.S. citizens are six per cent
of world's population consuming sixty
per cent of world's resources. Had
Americans been born pigs rather than men,
it would not have been different.
Finding one of them acceptable, people
say, "You're not like an American."
She said people she talked to about the
global services (and the notion
services'd bring about global living
without war) said : Yes, of course,
that's right. But how is it going
to happen? **Deep drilling : a slight**
angle and without meaning to you're
taking oil from under someone else's
property. Erik Satie's Venetian
gold merchant : He hugs the bag of gold,
takes some pieces out, kisses them,
carefully putting them back. After other
financial-erotic acts, not being able
to resist, he gets into the bag
himself. Coming out of it somewhat later,
he discovers he has a headache. LXII. We
open our eyes and ears seeing life
each day excellent as it is. This
realization no longer needs art though
without art it would have been difficult
(yoga, zazen, etc.) to come by.
Having this realization, we gather
energies, ours and the ones of
nature, in order to make this intolerable
world endurable. **Robots.** **Ivan**
Sutherand : ". . . it is not enough for
a computer to print an answer. The
answer is useful only when it leads

to new human understanding . . . Widespread use of graphic inputs and outputs with computers will bring about a major increase in scientific engineering, and educational productivity." **LXIII. We talked about Gaudi. Mies van der Rohe admired the Gaudi buildings in and near Barcelona and the Park Güell. Laura said that driving to the apartment from the office Mies was misanthropic. He had said that there are too few good people in the world.** (Duchamp talking about the human mind **pointed out how poorly it** works.) Isolate aspect of human nature which brought it about no one (not even those devoted to his work) knows how many pieces of Satie's *Furniture Music* were written or where they are. Call it collective thoughtlessness. There exist, we're told, unused areas of the brain. They should be put to work. LXIV. Days spent hunting for non-synthetic foods. At sunset become artists in the kitchen. Other days spent making something inedible (painting, theatre, etc. and the sciences), paying attention to things already made (classics, history, humanities). **Plastics.** *Waddington : ". . . the richness of individual life depends to a major extent on constructive enterprises . . . which are on such a large scale that only society as a whole can undertake them."* **Effortless speed (seven hundred and fifty miles per hour) :**

people blown through tunnels downhill from
Boston to New York. Effortless slowing
down : tunnel goes uphill. Asked about
religion he said he never said anything
against it : "It's the only thing that
keeps people in line." What about
art? Is art, formerly religion's servant,
now, without out realizing it, a kind of
policing activity? We need a purely
secular morality. LXV. Pia Gilbert,
born in southern Germany, got in a
taxicab in New York City. The driver
said, "I'm a Black Muslim." She
replied, "I'm sorry to hear it." "You
don't believe in the truth?" "That
isn't the truth." "You don't like
Negroes?" "What makes you think I'm not
a Negro?" What it is is a field. Looks
like we'll have networks in that
field. Lines crisscrossing on a
multiplicity of levels. There'll be, as
ever, the nothing-in-between. Wrist
watches with alarms that tell us as we
travel around when we should eat (not
when the airline hostess gives us
food, but when, according to our own
systems, we should have it). New function
for doctors : adjusting our wrist
alarms. LXVI. "They dance the world as
it will be . . . is now when they
dance." Technique. Discipline.
Ultimately it's not a question of
taste. It's the other way around.
Each thing in the world asks us, "What
makes you think I'm not something you

like?" The use of drugs to facilitate religious experience is against the stream of the times. (He lost interest in the tape-music center, its experiments and performances. He went to the Southwest desert. He removed himself from the others.) **Begging : difficult profession. In India, parents maim children producing bodies that'll attract pity. His eyes are sheep's eyes; his mind's superb. Decided not to give him a penny. Then did (after reading letter Satie'd written shortly before death, asking for a little money, enough so he could sit in a corner, smoke his pipe).** *LXVII. Asked the Spanish doctor what she thought about the human mind in a world of computers. She said computers are always right but life isn't about being right.* Pia's defense of property was touching. As she explained, she and people she knew had suffered at the hands of others. She said that by means of things they like and acquire people position themselves with respect to society. Duchamp : Property is at the base of it. Until you give up owning property radical social change is impossible. We ought either to get rid of God or to find Another Who doesn't permit mention of trust in Him on pieces of money. Or taxation could be augmented to the point where no one has any money at all. In which case we could keep God. LXVIII. DEFINITION

OF THE WORD "COSMOPOLITAN" : 1.
BELONGING TO ALL THE WORLD. **2. At home
in any country; without local or
national attachments. 3. Composed
of elements gathered from all or
various parts of the world.** BERTRAND
RUSSELL ASKS AMERICAN CITIZENS : CAN YOU
JUSTIFY YOUR GOVERNMENT'S USE IN VIETNAM
OF POISON CHEMICALS AND GAS, THE
SATURATION BOMBING OF THE ENTIRE
COUNTRY WITH JELLY-GASOLINE AND
PHOSPHORUS? NAPALM AND PHOSPHORUS
BURN UNTIL THE VICTIM IS REDUCED TO
A BUBBLING MASS. *Ramakrishna said :
Given a choice between going* **to heaven
and hearing a lecture on heaven, people
would choose the lecture.
Electronic Sketching. Engineers
Focus Light on Screen to Design Visually
via Computer.** LXIX. Sir Charles Dodds :
". . . assume that cancer and
cardiovascular problems are solved.
. . . We shall see institutions filled
with scientists of many biological
disciplines devoting their time to a
study of the ageing process." He says
no evidence exists that age
accompanied by degeneration is or
isn't a natural process. Every
death may have been unnatural, due to
extraneous causes. **Lecture series on
War (a summit series) : lectures to
be given by heads of states saying
whatever they will on the general
subject of fighting and why one does**

doesn't do it. **Disgust.** **Any proverbs that pass through our heads should be examined in a spirit of skepticism, their opposites in some cases reinforced, e.g., instead of "A rolling stone gathers no moss" establish "He doesn't let the grass grow under his feet."** *LXX.* *Something needs to be done about the postal services. Either that or we should stop assuming just because we mailed something it will get where we sent* **it.** NOT JUST HEADS OF STATE FOR LECTURE SERIES ON War, but heads of corporations too. Let it become household knowledge that being employed by such and such a company is no different from being drafted for such and such **a battlefront.** "Now's the time. Never this opportunity again (plans for centennial celebration : funds available)." Including in our awareness whatever's/whoever's exterior to our focus of attention. In this way eliminating the practices involving guilt/aggression/conscience, "turning our backs," John R. Seeley, "on an anal and phallic world to bring into being a reign of genitality (enjoyment by others must be a condition of one's own enjoyment)." **LXXI.** **Fire.** *Not unpleasing additions to water, but the subtraction from it of noxious elements.* **American school-teacher in Japan, having been assured she could have a private bath, told attendant she'd**

arranged to be alone. He said, "I'm here to see that you are." *Art instead of being an object made by one person is a process set in motion by a group of people. Art's socialized. It isn't someone saying something, but people doing things, giving everyone (including those involved) the opportunity to have experiences they would not otherwise have had. Indians in northern Saskatchewan, farmers in L'Isle de France, they've all forgotten what wild plants are edible. I was talking about this loss with Père Patrice. He said they've also forgotten how to sing. LXXII. The children have a society of their own. They have no need for ours. At the airport Ain said he came* **simply to see whether** his mother was all right. *Mumma's music* (Mesa) *for Cunningham's dance called* Place. *Sitting in the audience I felt afterword as though I'd been rung through a ringer. Then had to play Satie's* Nocturnes, *something not easy for me to do. Wrong notes all over the place. Tonight the program's being repeated. I've practiced. I'll be deaf and blind. Experimentation. Summit lecture series on War : not to be given in one city, but via a global Telstar-like facility, each receiving set throughout the world equipped with a device permitting hearing no matter what speech in one's own tongue.* **LXXIII.**

Progress. Since for long we've been saying that money is the root of all evil, we should get rid of it, lock, stock **and barrel.** *Take all the people who are now living in the world, McLuhan told me. Stand them up. Jammed together, they'd fit into the New York City subway system. I asked the skin-doctor why skin-doctors do such poor work. "Oh," he said, "We don't do any worse than the other doctors : it's just that you can see the results of our work."* Portuguese lady mentioned Lieh-tzu. Story : man, walking out of stone cliff through fire, astonishing those who saw him, was asked how he did it. "What?" Came out of stone, walked through fire. "I know nothing," he said, "about either of those *two things."* LXXIV. Ephemeralization. Away from the earth into the air. Or : "on earth as it is in heaven." More with less : van der Rohe (aesthetics) : Fuller (society of world men). Nourishment via odors, life maintained by inhalation : August Comte (*Système de Politique Positive,* second volume). Individuality. Out of the darkness of psychoanalysis into sunny behavioral psychology (people picking up their couches and walking). **U.S. highway diner : now that I haven't eaten the potatoes, they will throw them away (they should have been thrown away before being served). Rich, we become richer. No way once it**

begins to impede accumulation.
Universe. They've put the cart before the horse : they're better about publicity than they are about what they publicize. *LXXV. Sometimes the truth gets out : years ago the double-spread in a New York newspaper showing the faces of the forty or so men (industrialists) who rule the world. All of her children were male, twelve of them. "She should be studied, " Duchamp said. "She is the solution of a problem." A suite for two.* **Instead of transformation into** OTHER FORMS (REINCARNATION) REGENERATION OF EACH INDIVIDUAL. PRECEDENT : **constant remaking of Shinto temples** *in* **Japan. (With his thumbnail Tudor kept the bass-string in** vibration.) Include changes in design : invention applied to a living body. **(Electronics : reincarnation without hiatus of death.)** Rembrandt. **We have everything we used to have. The Mona Lisa's** still with us for instance. On top of which we have the Mona Lisa with a mustache. We have, so to speak, more than we need. LXXVI. Electric clothing. **The program was changed.** *We need news. Not just bad news : good news and news that's neither good nor bad. Heads of state lecturing on war (knowing they are speaking to people all over the world) will not be able to promote national objectives. We were impatient. So, we telephoned to*

find out whether the bus was coming, even though the appointed hour had not yet struck. **Figuéras. Looking for corduroy suit, noticed chamber pots, each with eye and inscription at the base of the bowl, the eye primitively painted with brilliant** *colors. The Catalan inscription was black :* ***I* see thee.** LXXVII. He refuses to give up. When he walks across the room, you wonder whether he's going to make it (a strange orientation of the upper body in relation to the legs, an original way of putting one foot in front of the other). *Out of Illinois into Sweden. (How will it happen? Will we do it or will it be done to us? Unemployment.) Climate control. Stravinsky's objection to Schoenberg's music : it isn't modern (too much like, though more interesting than, Brahms'). Absence of* **modernity's effect of Schoenberg's accepting tradition, hook, line and sinker. Sounds everywhere. Our** concerts celebrate the fact concerts're no longer necessary. *LXXVIII. The rehearsals continued and more concerts were given. Her playing which had been superb became merely correct. It was necessary to suggest a certain sloppiness, the playing of something that hadn't been written. Computer-made music (synthesized* Blue Moon*) presented same problem. Random elements introduced.* **Dad's cold remedy (a**

cure-all combining menthol, thymol in alcohol : Cowell preferred it to whiskey), Dad's inhaler for quick introduction to blood stream of vitamins, hormones. American Medical Association prevented general marketing of these products. *The doctor telephoned to ask whether Grandfather was still alive. Turned out that instead of analyzing Grandfather's urine he had studied some apple juice that Grandmother had given the hospital messenger when he came to pick up the sample.* **LXXIX. Get it, she said, so it's unknown which parent conceiving will bear the child. Responsibility undefined. Circa one hundred and seventy-five kinds of male, sixty, seventy kinds of female. Sterility. He had actually gotten slides showing the passage of the gene from one cell to the next. Destruction. Reconstitution.** *(What we want is very little, nothing, so to* speak. **We just want those things that have so often been promised or stated : Liberty,** Equality, Fraternity; Freedom of this and that.) *Clothes for entertainment, not because of shame. Privacy to become an unusual rather* than expected experience. **Given disinfection, sanitation, removal of social concerns re defecation, urination. No self-consciousness. Living like animals, becoming touchable.** LXXX. Ancient

Chinese imperial decree : Burn the books! To have the books that are not yet written, prohibit reading the ones on shelves. Fire takes place of dust producing beneficent ashes. Tried conversation (engineers and artists). Found it didn't work. At the last minute, our profound differences (different attitudes toward time?) threatened performance. What changed matters, made conversation possible, produced cooperation, reinstated one's desire for continuity etc., were *things*, dumb inanimate things (once in our hands they generated thought, speech, action). *Say lecture series on war cannot be arranged. Rule that summit meetings must be made public via TV, satellite, the works. Increase frequency of summit meetings. One way or another, that is, let the game be shown for what it is to those having time and interest to observe it.* LXXXI. Shirley Genther's arranging for me to receive the *Kaiser Reports.* You don't pay for them. They just come in the mail. Speakers for lecture series : *Mao Tse-Tung, Ho Chih Minh, some African Bushman, Nikita K., LBJ, Charles de Gaulle, etc.* We now expect a good deal (that the lights will turn on, the telephone will work, etc.), what we want is a comfortable bed (each one of us has a different notion of comfort), fresh air, delicious water, fine food, wine (there again, we differ). Into the night : the days to come. Barbara said she'd heard the political situation in some South American country being what it was (bizarre, dishonest and meaningless), a gorilla in the zoo was nominated and elected President.

LXXXII. In music it was hopeless to think in terms of the old structure (tonality), to do things following old methods (counterpoint, harmony), to use the old materials (orchestral instruments). We started from scratch : sound, silence, time, activity. In society, no amount of doctoring up economics/politics will help. Begin again, assuming abundance, unemployment, a field situation, multiplicity, unpredictability, immediacy, the possibility of participation. *Schools we'll live in (their architecture). Spaces without partitions. Noticing what the others are doing (they also think). Giving no thought to graduation. We know it's a melody but it's one we've not yet sung.* Power of momentum.

LXXXIII. There are those of course who have no time for improving the world. They are struggling to keep it going. Disciplines that require exercise. *Lunch in Chicago : She asked* me whether it was true that art no longer interested me. I said I thought we'd done it (opened our eyes, our ears). What's urgent is society. Not fixing it but changing it so it works. Self-service. Time for anger. Miscegenation : generation of a lasting biochemical change. We gave up judgments, substituted poetry. **Fire engines in the street below. Smoke** *in the halls. Called the desk. They said* there was no cause for alarm. LXXIV. *"If you and Daddy get a divorce, I'm not going to go with you and I'm not going to go with Daddy." His mother said, "Where would you go then?" "I'd go back to nature."* **North Pole is on the** *move : used to be in the Philippines.* They give us food because we're traveling by air. Pretty soon they'll do the same even when we're on the ground (trip or no trip). We have only one mind (the one we share). Changing things radically, therefore, is simple. You just change that one mind. Base human nature on allishness (soon **enough global** selfishness will become something to **think about).** LXXXV. Political steps restricted to those taken in front of television cameras, so people everywhere can see where they're going. Better yet : politicians take no political steps alone. Politicians (via TV) simply make suggestions. Receiving sets equipped with transmission means enabling people to vote on whether or not a proposed step or steps should be taken. Denial of what one's believed in.

Amplification of the sound of feet,
feet one sees walking. [Talked about
disintegrating passenger at one end of
line, reassembling him at his
destination. Pittsburgh Skybus : push a
button : following a path, bus goes where
you wanted it to go. Northwest plans
for shooting people through tunnels with
compressed air. Graduated speeds for
Sychroveyor travel. Insisted on
private transportation (possibly
electrical : getting home, plug in car :
unused, it gets recharged).] **LXXXVI.**
The lazy dog (a bomb containing ten
thousand slivers of razor-sharp
steel). In one province of North
Vietnam, the most densely populated, one
hundred million slivers of razor-sharp
steel have fallen in a period of
thirteen months. These razor darts
slice the villagers to ribbons. Maki
thinks Hawaii's another part of
Japan. Portugal thinks of Angola
not as a colony but as Portugal.
U.S.A. thinks Free World is U.S.A.'s
world, is determined to keep it free,
U.S.A.-determined. **The possibility**
of conversation resides in the
impossibility of two people having
the same experience whether or not their
attention is directed one-pointedly. An
ancient Buddhist realization (sitting
in different seats). *LXXXVII. Exhaustion.*
Sleep disturbed by dream. Said we were
to have regular tours each year, four of

them, each to last four months.
First one : performance in Alaska,
NORTH POLE, RUSSIA, FINLAND. Parking at
the super-market, she changed her
plan, gathering lamb's quarters, **mushrooms,**
and horseradish she'd noticed growing wild
outside. *Earth a city as Paris was :*
people seen in love on the streets.
Electric clothes rechargeable at public
couches, couches provided with
adjustable domes, domes raised or lowered
according to the weather, cataclysmic
events foreseen and observed as theatre
from a distance, distance provided by
immediate mass transportation.
Disease removed, the use of faeces,
animal and human, to enrich the earth
(economy, no refuse). *Starting over again*
from the point of human well-being,
non-fluent factors in the exchange
between man and universe (detergents
for instance) disused. A new
ecology. The enjoyment of "dirt".
("Hands.") LXXXVIII. The woods : finding a
cabin nobody's living in. It'll be
fun fixing it up. Details of *dawn*
observed, unstudied. **Success.** **All**
desires gratified, we say No but smile at
the same time (taking a rain check).
Blessed are the misers : *they shall give*
what they have to others. *The girls in*
the cities were forced into teams of
prostitutes for U.S. troops. *The Saigon*
government forced literally tens of
thousands of young girls into camps for

U.S. troops. Armistice November Eleventh. When's Second World War's Armistice? Need three hundred and sixty-three more wars arranged so each ends on a different day, entire year becoming one Armistice after another. Wars cold rather than hot. Lectures on war preferable to war itself. Annual celebration of ends of lectures, each and every day. LXXXIX. Society, not being a process a king sets in motion, becomes an impersonal place understood and made useful so that no matter what each individual does his actions enliven the total picture. Anarchy (no laws or conventions) in a place that works. Society's individualized. The doctor didn't know what the disease was. It attacked everyone differently, wherever a person was vulnerable. **Into that world when it's changed things'll reenter we'd renounced, e.g. value judgments (cf. the dominant seventh). They'll not monopolize nor suggest what happens next. (He hit her over the head the mother who'd lost her only child, saying, "This will give you something to cry about.") Constant lamentation. (We cry because anyone's head was struck.) Tears : a global enterprise.** XC. President Eisenhower (1953) : Let us assume we lost Indo-China. If Indo-China goes, the tin and tungsten we so greatly value would cease coming. We are after the

cheapest way to prevent the occurrence
of something terrible—the loss of
our ability to get what we want from
the riches of the Indo-Chinese
territory and from Southeast Asia. If
we get through 1972, Fuller says, we've
got it made. 1972 ends the present
critical period. Following *present
trends, fifty per cent of the world's
population will then have what they need.
The other fifty per cent will rapidly
join their ranks. Say by the year 2000.*

Diary: How to Improve the World (You Will Only Make Matters Worse) Continued 1968 (Revised)

XCI. Laughter. Computer music. No one mentions secrecy. Machine language. Accumulation of sub-routines, sub-routines anyone may use. Truth's not true. We were speaking of individuality (Thoreau's "respect for the individual") : Brown connected 'atom' with 'individual' (they've both been split). An individual, having no separate soul, is a time-span, a collection of changes. Our nature's that of Nature. Nothing's fixed. Excepting everything, there's nothing to respect. He'd go along, Brown said, with "the here and the now." **Why, in recent wars, does U.S. favor the south against the north? Non-strategic. Fight *against* the south : South, say Africa, siding with African nations to the north. Whites giving their lives for blacks! Soldiers would return victorious, pockets full of diamonds.** *XCII. June 23. (1840) "We Yankees are not* so far from right,"—(Thoreau)—"who answer one question by asking another. Yes and No are lies. A true answer will not aim to establish anything, but rather to set all well afloat." **Mentioning opposites, he called** them correlatives. Fuller calls them complements. Taking down the fences. Frontiers describe what's beyond as well as enclosed.

Three. **I noticed the nurses were kind to her. "Naturally they are. If you like people, they like you."** **When I**

received the letter that said I'd be
required to sign a form stating I
didn't want to overthrow the
government (otherwise I wouldn't get
the position I'd been offered), I asked
my friends what to do. They said : Sign
the form; take the job; go on with your
work. **XCIII. The Israeli-Arab**
situation's hopeless. Jewish friends
I talked *to didn't make good sense.*
Quote : After ages suffering, **aren't**
you glad we finally have a little
success? Unquote. Suggesting Jews
use technological know-how to benefit
Arabs, I was given this reply : Israelis
wanted to. ARABS *wouldn't let 'em.*
Weather changed. It's freezing. In
no time AT ALL THE TEMPERATURE
DROPPED A TOTAL OF FORTY DEGREES.
Uglification. We're good at it.
Single individuals without
encountering obstacles darken the corners
where they are. When Gandhi was asked what
he thought of Western Civilization, he
said, "It would be nice." One thing we
refuse is to employ an answering
service. It's of the greatest urgency—a
matter of ethics even—that we be able to
reach one another. Those who are
selfish will change their minds re
interruptions (i.e. become
superficially ethical) : incoming telephone
calls will be the means by which one's
social credit exceeds a basic economic
security (social usefulness
measured). XCIV. When I entered the

house, I noticed some very interesting music was being played. After a drink or two, I asked my hostess what it was. She said, "You can't be serious?" **Scientists are sometimes not scientific. Take atomic garbage. First they put it in rivers and streams. Then someone noticed the waters began to boil. Now just as cats do after shitting, scientists dig a trench, put the garbage in it, cover it up, and then forget about it.** **Ecological thinking.** "Decisions **to make."** **There must be times for him, as there are for me, when, looking in my direction expecting to say hello, I pass by preoccupied. Artificial death (something we invented).** XCV. Coal and oil we use are being replenished. Fossilization. It takes ages. Buckminster Fuller, speaking in financial terms, describes underground energy sources as capital sources **to differentiate them from those above ground which he describes as income. Fuller advises saving capital for emergencies.** Changed, mind includes even itself. Unchanged, nothing gets in or out. I was grounded. The pilot refused to fly. I took to the woods. Found *Tricholoma equestre* (first time I ever did). Then in Ohio, on the way to another airport, found *Pleuroti, Collybiae.* Revolution. **Two people making same kind of music is one music too many.** XCVI. Unripe **fruit.**

Asked Fuller about atomic energy. He
didn't smile. His comment : It's partly
income, partly capital. I was given a
book of photographs and poems. The
photographs're *nineteen inches wide,*
only a few inches high. They are shots
of the Midwest. Going to Illinois, I
took this book along as aesthetic
insurance against the land and air
I'd **be living in. In the course of telling**
what she'd seen while traveling around
the world, Mrs. Cunningham mentioned the
camels in Japan. Mr. Cunningham said,
"You must mean the camels in Egypt."
Going on, Mrs. Cunningham said
parenthetically, "Of course that's what I
mean." XCVII. Music (not
composition). The U.S. government
has joined the protest movement.
Postage stamp bears the motto : Search
for Peace. Another commemorates
Thoreau. (Wanderers. No notion of where
we'll be **going next.)** *Driving to*
Chicago, no need for art. Land's an
ocean. Earth's black. Trees, even
those with leaves, visible. Pheasants,
frightened, run the road from China.
Spring sponges. Fall stumpies and
quirines. Pinkies. He got his hands dirty
so we could live. (We, too, are
trees.) That I'm grateful costs him no
time. Coming back from the pilgrimage,
they tell us the roof is leaking. It's
good our heads're worn-out. (His
ideas are getting in.) He's as serious and
frivolous as Chaos. **"When?" was the**

question she asked. Then added : "Each second counts." XCVIII. "Why'd you hit him in the first place?" "I didn't. I only hit him when he hit me back." *Moon. Tides.* Asked why the radios didn't work, she said, "We bought the big one for seventy-five dollars and it didn't work. Then we bought the little one. It doesn't work either, but it only cost ten dollars." **"Classification . . . ceases when it's no longer possible** *to establish* oppositions." (Government's outmoded.) **To improve society, spend more time** with *people whom you* **haven't met.** *Paul Goodman : "A man . . . draws now, as far as he can, on the natural force* in *him that is no different from what it will be in the new society . . . Merely continuing to exist and act in nature and freedom, a free man wins the victory, establishes the new society . . ."* *(Drawing the Line).* XCIX. We do what no one else does. Economy. (We do not believe in "human nature.") We are nouveau-riches. Beyond that, we are criminals. There, outside the law, we tell the truth. For this reason, we exploit technology. **Circumstances determine our actions.** Wind. Straw that will break Christmas's **back : we'll already have what someone intends to give** *us.* **Friendship.** The price-system and government that enforces it are on the way out. They're going out the way a fire *does.* Protest actions fan the flames of a dying fire. Protest helps to keep the government going. **Energy from outer space. Radioaction in a form not requiring fission/fusion. C. She bought a number of towels to give as Christmas presents to people in the community. By mistake she gave them all to me. Violence. If revolution's colored, include white. White and black look well together. Gentle Thursday. My plan was to do my work and then join Cincinnati's Be-In. At 4:30 Andy telephoned to say it had petered out. Predictions of astrologers. "The start of a deep transformation on earth." We're leaving the Piscean age, entering the Aquarian one. We'll be living in a situation of overlap, interplay, global unity, universal understanding, collective peace and harmony. Subjectivity.** Kill two birds with one stone. Stop using oil and coal. We'll keep them in the earth against a rainy day. Large cause of air-pollution'll be eliminated. We'll use energies above ground—sun, wind, tides. Air'll automatically become what it was : something good to breathe. **CI. Sri Ramakrishna not only lived as a man, a woman, a monkey : he lived for six months as a plant, standing on one leg in ecstasy.** *We are not arranging things in order (that's the function of the utilities) : we are merely facilitating processes so that anything can happen.* **After leaving Tokyo's** airport, Itu Hisuki wrote this letter : "Mr. Baggage Man American Airlines United States of Los Angeles Gentleman dear sir : I damn seldom where my suitcase are. She no fly. You no more fit to baggage master than for crysake that's all I hope. What's the matter you? Itu Hisuki" **CII. We think** at the same time others (animates, inanimates) think. We are intimate in advance with whatever will happen. Not blood. Just relationship. **Power and profit structures're out of cahoots with current technology. Aware of new inventions, corporations put them aside, waiting for competitive reasons until they're obliged to use new gimmicks. Possessed of the atom bomb, they are hog-tied. They dare not use it. Alice. Wonderland.** *Robert Duncan told me his poetry was picked up from other people. The only time he felt, he said, like using quotation marks was when the words he wrote were his.* Say the country's based on law and order as after each riot politicians maintain. Instead of allocating funds for summer entertainments in Roman efforts to distract the masses, it would be more effective to prohibit advertising (TV commercials in particular) so that the poor wouldn't know what it was they were missing. CIII. She'd been born in her summer home overlooking a mountain lake formerly owned by her family, now

shared with Boy Scouts. Carpenter whom she'd employed, whom she'd known since childhood, always treated her like an outsider. While he rested, she asked, "What's the difference between natives and outsiders?" "Natives," he replied, "eat indoors and shit outdoors, outsiders eat outdoors and shit indoors." *Our flights are interrupted by overnight stays in airport motels. No one knows where we are. McLuhan said it. We're like the Middle Ages. People building cathedrals. Glorification. No need for God : just Universe.* **Doing something we don't know how to do. No technique. Dad used to say : If someone says "Can't," that indicates the thing for you to** do. *CIV. Spent several hours searching through a book trying to find the idea I'd gotten out of it. I couldn't find it. I still have the idea.* X. *He said he'd never heard my music. "You haven't missed a thing." Letter to Tenney : It's useless to play lullabies for those who cannot go to sleep. Retaliating, they'll put you in prison. We'll have lost synergetic advantage working* with you gave us. (How many are we? You also benefited.) You're right, of course (they're wrong). But you don't intend, do you, to perpetuate such distinctions? First thing he did after taking the job as school principal was to sign his resignation, explaining he didn't want people to feel obliged to keep him around. Then he fired the librarian, permitting students free access to books. Instead of being stolen or not returned, inventory after one year showed there were fifty more books than there had been originally. CV. "Common Sense." *We do what we do by means of contradiction.* Gravity's a local event, one of many in the electrostatic field. Find means whereby one can tune in or out of **the gravitational field of this or that body in space. (Nonviolent space travel.) Find other uses of gravity for those who're living on Earth. Consider incestuous any marriage between two people of the** same race, country or faith. **No idea how it happens. Even if we had an idea (which's been shown to facilitate its escaping our notice) it'd still happen. Met John Platt.** He suggests that contraceptive substances be added **to basic foods : flour, rice, sugar, salt, etc. The human species would become normally unreproductive. Should a couple wish to have a child, they'd go to special stores to procure their food. Every child a wanted child. CVI. Hard** CLAY THE EARTH/ IRON-WEED THE CORN/ THAT WAS MY CRIB (Teeny fifteen years old) If the situation is hopeless, we have nothing to worry about. Post-graduate studies. Quantum Theory. January. Drove across Ding Darling Sanctuary on Sanibel off Florida's

western coast. Saw vulture; hawks;
ducks and smaller birds; white, blue,
black and grey taller birds, poised on
branches or stalking the shallow waters.
Man got out of his car behind us to
photograph. We asked him what kind of
bird it was. He said, "That's a grey
heron, five feet tall." During the
discussion, she asked a question
about education. Answer : People together
without restrictions in a situation
abundantly implemented. She asked another.
"People to whom it never occurs to ask :
Mother! What shall I do *now?" She
turned and left the room. CVII. Hands
aren't possessive. They belong to the
same body. They taught us art was
self-expression. You had to have
"something to say." They were wrong :
you don't have to say anything. Think of
the others as artists. Art's
self-alteration.* ("Charlotte
Thrasher came to me late last evening
to say that she'd jumped a wave,
taken the way of the fishes and would
not return until morning.") *If we
start with the past and move to the
present, we go from pleasure to*
irritation. Do you know what's happening?
The Indian mind is moving. It'll
handle computers, cybernetics,
what-have-you, better than other
minds can. CVIII. Global Civil War.
**Family as it now stands doesn't work.
North, south, brothers are quarreling,
running to one parent or the other**

to obtain a favorable judgment. A mother telephoned to ask whether her son **was coming home for Christmas. "No," he replied, "I love you, but** *I'm going west. You and Dad're always bickering."* Examine thoughts and words, written or spoken, weeding out those that are dead. Dead ones are those concerning aggression. Konrad Lorenz : the evolution of human nature. **Toshi Ichiyanagi says : Funny thing about that Itu Hisuki story** *is that Itu Hisuki* **is not a very Japanese name. CIX. Reading Thoreau's** ***Journal*****, I discover any idea I've ever had worth its salt.** *(Oppressive laws were made to keep two Irishmen from fighting in the streets.)* The door opened. He walked in, turned on the light, sat down, died. The light is still on. No one turned it off. India : a luxury we can no longer afford. **Graves said : Imagine that you're dreaming. I told Ellen to stretch her visit to the limit, then stay another** *day.* GOVERNMENT'S CONTEMPORARY IF ITS ACTIVITIES AREN'T INTERRUPTED BY THE ACTION OF TECHNOLOGY. AMERICANS, TO REMAIN RICH, STRONG, REQUIRED TO CURTAIL WORLD TRAVEL, STOP INVESTMENT IN FOREIGN INDUSTRIES. ERGO : WASHINGTON'S BEHIND THE TIMES. **CX. At the present moment, the question is : Do I have enough change for another beer? More important question : Is there enough food and** drink for everyone who **is living? Civilization is Hamletized**

(people are dying right and left) : To be or not to be. That is the question. *Tempo no longer exists. Just quantity. Say there are only a few sounds. Say they're loud. What to do? Jump?* **"But still Vietnam goes on! And what of the concentration camps in California, etc? . . . Who shall be called to serve 'their country' in** *them . . . ? Malcolm"* Criticism's not the time to think. Think ahead of time. Buckminster Fuller. **CXI. Tenney wrote** to say : "What's required . . . is . . . radical eclecticism (Ives) . . . 'every composer's duty' . . . More power to Fuller . . . to *revolutionary guerillas . . . to Christian pacifists . . . to flower children . . . to hippies . . . acidheads . . . beatniks, diggers and provos . . . to the militant blacks . . . to those who keep asking questions." We were at opposite ends of the hall. We left our separate rooms and are now in the hall itself.* Problems of governments are not inclusive enough. We need (we've *got them) global problems in order to find global solutions. Problems connected with sounds were insufficient to change* the nature of music. We had to conceive of silence in order to open our ears. We need to conceive of anarchy to be able whole-heartedly to do whatever another tells us to. CXII. It's been dangerous. Still is. Warnings are constantly given. Furthermore, though we gave our lives, our actions seemed superficial.

That is, we went out rather than in.
Premise was : opposites are intimately
connected. Were we to start again,
we'd start from a consideration
(constellation of ideas). What we
have would be no uglier called by
another name. Veblen called it the
price-system. Mills called it the Power
Elite. It's probably no more than
ninety-nine people who don't know what
they're doing. They're involved in
high finance. Fascinating form of
gambling. We sent music outdoors as
one sends children to play, so
grown-ups could get what they were
doing done. *CXIII. McHale : "The . . .
interdependence of all nations . . . to
maintain . . . daily* operations (of airlines,
telecommunications and other . . . global
services), now renders ineffective . . .
attempts at unilateral action based on
imaginary sovereign autonomy. We
are . . . hypnotized by such notions . . .
though they are no longer operable
in the real world. When we went by
mail-boat to visit Fuller, the fog was so
thick you couldn't see where you were
going. That night he talked by
candlelight. In the morning the fog had
lifted. All the islands of the Penobscot
were visible, even the ones in the
distance. It was like Matsushima, but
larger. We'll keep the Stop and Go signs—
even their colors : red and green.
But we'll give the signs the ability
to observe traffic so that the Go sign

will not appear when there are no cars waiting to go. *CXIV. Sleep's what we need. It produces an emptiness in us into which sooner or later energies flow. Metabolism.* **Combine nursing homes with** nursery schools. Bring very old and very young **together : they interest one another.** **Farting, don't think, just fart.** SIGN ABOVE THE TOILET : **Have patience! The** toilet *will* flush. *Just give it time to fill up.* Artilleryman, flying home, anxious to return to Vietnam, said there's a job to be done. If soldiers were free to kill anyone anytime anywhere, war, he said, could be won. Army rules cramp our style. E.g., rubber trees aren't to be damaged in any way. CXV. Books one picked up and put down over a period, say, of ten years, picking them up on the eleventh to discover the impossibility of putting them down. What's the arithmetic of this? **The heavenly city's no longer** *walled-in : it has gone up in space.* **Talking about education, Fuller said he preferred talking to people whose minds weren't, say, more than half-filled up. Furthermore, a child, he said, by the mere fact of being born *is* educated. We're no longer willing to be entertained piecemeal—recitals of this and that, megalopolitan museums here and there. We insist on continuous use of aesthetic faculty.** *CXVI. Computers're bringing about a situation*

that's like the invention of harmony.
Sub-routines are like chords. No one
would think of keeping a chord to himself.
You'd give't to anybody who wanted it.
You'd welcome alterations of it.
Sub-routines are altered by a single punch.
We're getting music made by man himself :
not just one man. **STZ. Some**
programming errors arise from successive
operations without recourse between to
zero (an error that wasn't recognized
as such in 12-tone music). Neti-Neti :
the "nothing-in-between."
Society'll work without fatal *error if*
(Thoreau) it's governed not at all.
Store zero. **Planes that are used in**
Vietnam are planes left over from a
previous war. A new bomber just in order
to get up in the air gets to a point
beyond its destination. You'd think that
our leadership would manage to keep
abreast of technological advance, and
choose adversaries who are
positioned at the proper distance. CXVII.
World body. *We learn nothing from the*
things we know. The taxi-driver
insisted people have to have other people
to hate. I remained silent. Before
I left the cab, he changed his tune.
Comprehensive design. Meister
Eckhart spoke of the soul's simplicity.
But Nature's complicated. We must get
rid of the soul or train it to deal
with countless numbers of things.
Likewise the ego, its dreams, its value
judgments. (We just might make it.)

Dharma is being revitalized by sense
perceptions and extensions of them.
Giving up true and false. **The mind, like
a computer, produces a print-out.
It's on the palms of our hands. CXVIII.
Why keep connecting him with "his"
work? Don't you see that he's a human
being, whereas his work isn't? If,** for
instance, you decided to kick his work and
him, you would, wouldn't you, have to
perform two actions rather than a
single one? The more he leaves his
work, the more usable it becomes (room
in it for others). *Study universe.
Arrange matters so things are where they
belong. Radioactive refuse? Belongs
out in space. Past a certain threshold,
it'll go of its own accord to the Sun.*
HE SAID SOMETHING. I UNDERSTOOD
SOMETHING. **Communication? Edwin
Schlossberg** and Jon Dieges conducted
a class in Design at the University
of Southern Illinois (Design in
Buckminster Fuller's sense). Students did
research and wrote papers,
but gave them to one another instead of
handing them in to the teachers. At
the last session, one of the
students came up to Eddie and asked him
what his last name was.

Diary: How to Improve the World (You Will Only Make Matters Worse) Continued 1969 (Part V)

CXIX. No need to move the camera. (Pictures come to it.) Gather, Fuller advises, facts regarding human needs and world resources. Place in computer memory bank. Update continuously. Join team of programmers, competing to find speediest peaceful means for giving each world inhabitant what's needed for his kind of living. Videoize solution on football-field-sized geodesic world map, so fact continuously changing intelligent solution of world game exists becomes via TV household knowledge. **A study was made with computer to find out where in the world wealthy Americans prefer to retire. They retire, computer tells us, to Cuernavaca in Mexico, a hill town near Nairobi in Kenya, and some place or other in Nepal.** CXX. The goal is not to have a goal. **The new universe city will have no limits. It will not be in any special place. Having returned, as Fuller puts it, to** his **studies, teacher will be flying all over the world and even out into space.** Questions I might have learned to ask him can no longer **be** answered. Waiting in the hotel in Rio de Janeiro to hear whether or not I was to meet with the people who were studying anarchy (they had come in their studies to Thoreau and, having heard that I was enjoying Thoreau's *Journal*, had asked me to share with them

my thoughts) : telephone didn't ring.
CXXI. Act of sharing is a community act. Think of people outside the community. What do we share with them? Teacher played *hooky. Sent message : "Receiving instruction. Enjoying myself thoroughly. See you next week."* Lejaren Hiller's computer music project : "fantastic orchestra." Each sound to be a plurality of vibratory circumstances known or not known in nature. Impossible made possible. **Fuller : Nothing's artificial. It exists? It is natural.** How d'you manage to live with just one shirt? Before going to bed, I take a shower with my shirt still on. Afterwards I scrub the cuffs and collar with my electric toothbrush. Then I turn on the TV, hang my shirt on it. Best place I've found to dry it. **CXXII. Years ago zoological gardens began to get rid of wire fences, substituting means that decreased the sense of separation between animal and man. Coming back from The Junior Museum of Natural History in Sacramento, Billie Berton told me children now make applications for checking animals out. It took six weeks to teach the computer how to toss three coins six times. Somewhat worried, I tossed coins manually to discover from the I Ching how I Ching felt about being programmed. It was delighted.**

I Ching promised quantitative increase of benefits for culture. *What we've already done conspires against what we have now to do.* *CXXIII.* *Advice to Brazilian anarchists : Improve telephone* system. *Without telephone,* **merely starting revolution'll be impossible.** *Pinkville.* **Charles Peck. New York's State Botanist, spent most of his life with no place to work but a dark hallway. Just before he died the Government gave him a room with a window. Cadaqués : up around nine or ten; coffee; off by boat to** a cove where no others are; white wine, almonds, olives : chess, swimming, dominoes : back in town by one or two for lunch with him. (He had not been with us.) **Feared plan'd fail (no one wanted to get deeply involved). However, it worked. When disaster was imminent, people rose to occasion, did whatever was necessary to keep the thing going. (Reminder, not a revelation.)** He'd have **preferred silence to applause at the end (art instead of slap in the face.) CXXIV. Whispered truths. Looking for something irrelevant, I found I couldn't find it.** *"Wild as if we lived on . . . marrow of antelopes devoured raw." (Thoreau)* **Wanting to make some easy money, he took to cracking safes, was caught, put in penitentiary. While ill in the prison**

hospital, he had an affair with middle-aged
nurse. When he was released from
penitentiary, nurse introduced him to a
beautiful young girl whom he married.
His bride immediately inherited three
million dollars. College : two hundred
people reading same book. An obvious
mistake. Two hundred people can
read two hundred books. *Clothes I wear*
for mushroom hunting are rarely sent
to the cleaner. They constitute a
collection of odors I produce and
gather while rambling in the woods. I
notice not only dogs **(cats, too) are**
delighted (they love to smell me). *CXXV.*
Vacaville. **Spent the evening with** a
murderer. I asked him why he drank so
much coffee. He said, "There's
nothing else to do." University, which
now embraces studies formerly excluded
from it such as home economics,
music, and physical education, has
sister universities abroad, belongs
to consortium of universities here,
includes a "free" university. What's
adumbrated's indistinct from society
itself. Not a community of scholars
living like monks, but society
which works for any kind of living,
any kind of attention-placement, any
activity. *Something seems*
beautiful? Wittgenstein : You mean
it clicks? When things don't click,
take clicker from your pocket and
click it. CXXVI. Death. *Process*

involving Christmas trees takes place each year. Christmas trees that're grown in Hawaii are sent by freighter to be sold on the West Coast. Christmas trees that're grown on the West Coast are sent by freighter to be sold in Hawaii. *Ready or not, we are being readied. Complete checkup. I was more examined than ever before. Doctor's report: You're* very well except for your illnesses. **John McHale; "It has taken the history of mankind to produce the articles we have around us (the match, the computer): it is essential to see one sector of population isn't servicing another; we are all using** the same materials simultaneously; information storage never depletes; ability to **reuse materials makes us, after all these centuries, quite skillful."** *CXXVII.* **Impatience.** *Why do you have one TV set on top* OF THE OTHER? THE BOTTOM ONE DOESN'T **work.** There were fifty-two tapes. We had **to combine them for a single recording. We went to the studio where they could record eight at a time. When we had seventeen together it sounded like chamber music; when we had thirty-four together it sounded like** orchestral music; when we had fifty-two together it **didn't sound like anything we'd** *ever heard before.* **Milarepa.** LONDON PUBLISHER SENT BLANK ("FILL OUT.") SO I'D BE INCLUDED IN SURVEY OF

CONTEMPORARY POETS OF THE ENGLISH
LANGUAGE. THREW IT OUT. WEEK LATER
URGENT REQUEST PLUS DUPLICATE BLANK
ARRIVED. "PLEASE RETURN WITH A
GLOSSY PHOTO." COMPLIED. JULY, AUGUST,
SEPTEMBER. PUBLISHER THEN SENT
LETTER SAYING IT'D BEEN DECIDED I'M
NOT SIGNIFICANT POET AFTER ALL : IF I
WERE, EVERYONE ELSE'D BE TOO. **CXXVIII.**
Used to say "never the twain shall
meet." Now we don't hesitate to fight
oriental wars, there's no doubt about
usefulness of oriental thought for
western mind. Same's true for
Utopia. Its impracticality is no longer
to be assumed. Everything's changed.
Develop facilities that remove need
for middlemen. Soup cans are not only
beautiful (Warhol, for example) but true
(Campbell's soup is actually in them).
They're also constant reminders of
spiritual presence. "I am with you
always." Function fulfilled by
images of the Virgin Mary along a path
is now also fulfilled by the public
telephone. Instead of lighting a
candle, we insert a dime and dial. CXXIX.
Computer mistake in grade-giving
resulted in academic failure of
several brilliant students. After some
years the mistake was discovered.
Letter **was then sent to each student**
inviting him to resume his studies. Each
replied he was getting along very well
without education. Buddha reclines on his

right **side. So does the** lion. **How thorough he is! He told** *me his secrets. Town is very small, well-organized. Nothing can be found in it.* **An idea was given to them because they didn't have one. The** *Seychelles.* Cloth calendars for kitchen walls designed by Lois Long are sold throughout the U.S.A. Some years ago Lois made one by mistake giving two different dates to a single day : Thursday November 31 was also Thursday December 1. The calendar was very successful. **CXXX. Discipline (Disciple). Giving up one's country, all that's dear to one's country : "Leave thy father and mother . . ." Yoga (Yoke). Taming of the globe (Open :** In and Out). Einstein wrote to Freud to say men should stop having wars. Freud wrote back to say if you get rid of war you'll also get rid of love. Freud was wrong. What permits us to love one another and the earth we inhabit is that we and it are impermanent. We obsolesce. Life's everlasting. Individuals aren't. **A mushroom lasts for only a very short time. Often I go in the woods thinking after all these years I ought finally to be bored with fungi. But coming upon just any mushroom in good condition, I lose my mind all over again. Supreme good fortune : we're both alive!** *CXXXI. Things* **governments wish to divide between us**

belong to all of us : the land, for
instance, beneath the oceans.
People speak of literacy. But I, for one, can't read or write any computer language. Only numbers I know are those based on ten. I'm uneducated.
Home in Wayzata, Minnesota's very much like a home near Sitges (just south of Barcelona). Now we're itinerant there's no reason *to go on, for instance, picking fruit. Since we live longer, Margaret Mead says, we can change what we do. We can stop whatever it was we promised we'd always do and do something else.*
CXXXII. He is one of my closest friends.
HE ASKED ME FOR HELP. I GAVE IT.
He couldn't use it. TV Guide *tells what's going on, doesn't tell what we're obliged to look at. Where you are limits what channels you can receive.*
(Hearing sounds before they're audible is not the way to hear them.)
Imitate the telephones of your homes'n'highways. (Their indifference.) They aren't displeased when the person speaking is black. They aren't pleased when the person speaking is black. When lady in charge of university concerts asked what music day was to be called, I replied *Godamusicday.* She was delighted. Her husband, also affiliated with university (but in its **legal aspects), wasn't. "Profanity is forbidden. Nothing can be printed**

that might come to the Governor's notice." Duchamp, asked whether he believed in God : No. God is Man's stupidest idea. **CXXXIII. Traveling from one place to another we confine ourselves to the roads. That's why, of course, we feel so populated : we're too choosy about the space we use.** *Guests had left. Before going to bed, while reading a book he'd bought that morning, he chuckled. Ten minutes later, brushing his teeth, he died.* **Whole Earth. We connect Satie with Thoreau.** *Eleventh thunderclap?* **1928. Walter loved the Chinese, hated Communists. He couldn't bear the Japanese. Fortunately for Uncle, he died before the tables turned.** *Mushroom? Leaf?* **Backs** *ache. If we had immortal life (but we don't), it'd be reasonable to do as we do now : spend our time killing one another. CXXXIV. Chadwick, gardener at Santa Cruz. Nobby'd said, "You must meet our wizard." (Chadwick's back, Nobby told me, had been injured in war, but when we went mushrooming with his student-helpers, Chadwick, half-naked, leapt and ran like a pony. Catching up with him, it was joy and poetry I heard him speak. But while I listened he noticed some distant goal across and down the fields and, shouting something I couldn't understand because he'd already turned away, he was gone.)* **Students had defected**

from the university or had come especially from afar to work with him like slaves. They slept unsheltered in the woods. After the morning's hunt with him and them, I thought : These people live; others haven't even been born. CXXXV. IT WAS NOT QUITE MIDNIGHT. DUCHAMP WAS WAITING FOR US IN THE STREET. HE LOOKED FOR ALL THE WORLD LIKE A HANDSOME YOUNG MAN. **Want list of communes (places where Americans live who've given up dependence on power and possessions)? Write to Alternatives Foundation, 2441 Le Conte Ave., Berkeley, Calif., 94709 or to Carleton Collective Communities Clearinghouse,** Northfield, Minn., 55057. Future's no longer a secret. *Murderer asked, "What time is it?" "Nine o'clock." Five minutes later he repeated his question, "What time is it?"* **"Five minutes after nine." Ten.** *She had problem children. Their grades were so poor they couldn't enter college. I told her to stop worrying about them. She did. They've turned out beautifully. One married a Californian, has two fine sons, paints beautifully. Tucker's automobile expertise is in demand.* *CXXXVI. Talked about fact writing's less and less attractive. Picking up the pen, one knows idea's already entertained in other minds. Pen becomes absent. Sword'll follow suit. Flower Sermon.* **In the plane ready for last leg**

of flight to Yucatan (he'd flown from Berkeley, I from Palermo in Sicily). Grounded by fog we remained in Mexican plane three hours, which with subsequent flight gave me time to read Stent's typescript of his book, *The Coming of the Golden Age.* When questions came to mind, I simply put them to the author! Completely satisfied. How do you propose, Fuller was asked, to accomplish this without involvement in political action? His answer : The World Game provides an apolitical action, a solution no one's forced to accept. *When, however, you want it, you'll be* able, since you know it exists, to use it. CXXXVII. Puppy was eating his vomit. "That's one thing," his mistress said, "we don't do." Picked him up; put him outside; resumed her conversation. No one cleaned up the mess. (An elderly Viennese lady whose principal pleasure was listening to music was alarmed because she thought she was losing her hearing. She went to the doctor. He discovered her ears were full of wax. He removed it very easily.) *Man living in the Ojai knew how to manage unsheltered. But, hungry, he devised a plan that worked : to subtly change his environment* in terms of its seductiveness to picnickers so that coming upon it picnickers'd feel they'd made a discovery of the ideal place to

eat (he lived for years on food they
left behind). *CXXXVIII. Busy*
signal in the telephone system
sometimes means person one's calling's
talking to someone else. Sometimes busy
signal means someone else's trying to
reach very same person you're trying
to reach. This creates a problem.
Solution : two different types of busy
signals. If at some moment person
we're trying to reach (being called
before by someone else) answers,
genuine busy signal rings.
Presidential platform : promise
elected or not, to go on with my work,
not bothering about you; to remove
laws; to extend unlimited credit
throughout society regardless of
nationality. Observing distinctions
(race distinctions), side with underdog,
learning from him who was oppressed
to live outside the law not committing
crimes. Become slave to all there
is. (No need to become King.) Siding
with noises, musicians discovered
duration's impartiality. What
corresponds in society to sound's
parameter of duration? **CXXXIX.**
Vacation. This is ours. Don't just
"do your thing" : do so many things no one
will know what you are going to do next.
Add video screen to telephone. Give
each subscriber a thousand sheets of
recordable erasable material so
anytime, anywhere, anyone'd have

access to a thousand sheets of *something* (drawings, books, music, whatever). You'd just dial. If you dialed the wrong number, instead of uselessly disturbing another subscriber, you'd just **get surprising information, something unexpected. CXL. Statement by Stulman, manufacturer/ distributor of lumber products, founder/ President of the World Institute : The question before us is whether we will so organize the processes for gathering and applying knowledge that the creative powers of all men can be catalyzed for growth toward wholeness, or whether we will persist in our egocentric, ethnocentric, fact-accumulating, thing-oriented, power-amassing ways that are leading us to destruction.** Looking out the window into the forest, illuminated surfaces in the house (that aren't in the forest) are seen in the forest, 3-D in color. Hand that's placed on TV is placed at the same time outside on the tree. CXLI. The shower's in the room, not confined to a cubicle. On the opposite wall's a mirror. Steam from the hot water produces the slow disappearance of one's image. Pleasure of having a body, "Waiting for the gift from me to me of death." **Assassination of Martin Luther King. Apocalypse.** They have homes but they don't have the idea. Keep

Out. Languages separate people.
Images (TV, highway signs, trademarks, film) bring them together. Going
to the moon, we speak in numbers. A
year has passed. We pretend we can get
along without him. For three or four
years, Igor Stravinsky was treated for a
malady his doctors thought he had. When,
at death's door, Stravinsky's hands
turned black, the doctors concluded a
mistake had been made. CXLII.
That that's unknown brings mushroom
and leaf together. *"Ego dethroned." In
the course of being provided with
false teeth, Thoreau took ether. "You
are," he wrote, "told that it will
make you unconscious, but no one can
imagine what it is to be unconscious
until he has experienced it. If you
have an* **inclination to travel,
take," he advised, "the ether. You go
beyond the farthest star."** We know from
a variety of experiences that if we
have a sufficiently large number of
things, some or even many of them can be
bad but the sum-total is good for the
simple reason, say, that not all of
the things in it are good. CXLIII.
Found, page 74, in a book by Cassirer : it
is speech itself which prepares the way
whereby it is itself transcended.
From navigation to aviation. Fuller :
Renounce water as sanitation-means;
adopt compressed air (following
lead of dentists). Bits of hair and skin

floating in the air with pollen, seeds
and spores from plants. Out of water into
air and back to earth. I asked
Xenakis what's wrong with U.S.A. He
was quiet for a moment and then said,
"Too much power." **Put'em who threaten
possessions and power together with 'em who
offend our tastes in sex and dope.
Those who're touched, put'em in
asylums. Pack off old ones to
"senior communities," nursing homes. Our
children? Keep'em prisoner,
baby-sitter as warden. School? Good for
fifteen to twenty years. Army
afterward. Liberated, we live in prison.
No this, no that. Kill us before we
die!** CXLIV. We *have no icons : we
believe what we do.* *(Telephone
conversation turned towards politics.
Mrs.* **Emmons said she was certain
what the government was doing was
right. Beverly said, "How do you**
figure that?" Her mother replied,
"Well! This is a Christian country.") **We
leave food offerings for person who
makes next telephone call no matter
who he is : thus we transform highway
telephone booth into wayside shrine. I
don't believe, Duchamp said, in the
verb, to be. "I do not believe that I
am."** Commune problem : communes're
filled with gurus, needing (not having)
others "to guru." But teaching's
part'n'parcel of divisive society we're
leaving. *Thoreau : "My seniors have*

told me nothing . . . probably can tell me nothing to the purpose." **Davis : don't know what we're studying; don't know how we'll do it. Studied map. Should have taken road not on it** (went off to left). CXLV. Reprogramming. **Jack McKenzie's proposal : Set up alternative university program freeing a student from all curriculum responsibilities. Let him elect** his studies. When he leaves, give him, instead of degree, certificate telling what he did while in school. Looking at the sunset, Brown noticed part **of its beauty is caused by air pollution. Day after the assassination. Human being sitting at the table next to mine. Wanted to speak to him. Didn't. Didn't have the right.** AS WE LEFT THE VALLEY TO ENTER THE DESERT, I GAVE UP ALL THOUGHT OF FINDING mushrooms. But for some reason we stopped along the road. There underneath the pepper trees I found *Tricholoma personatum*, excellent, **in quantity. CXLVI. The poor? Where do *they* go to retire? Takilma, Oregon (America's third poorest town). Nothing to do : Free jam, peanut butter, staples. Have two children? Government'll give you two hundred and** forty dollars a month. Money comes through the mail. **Slight irritations ("make life sufficiently interesting to live") are provided by** visits of welfare worker whose assignment is Takilma. Takilma's beautiful. Problem in Takilma : Boredom. People often together sitting around talking. Let 'em close their mouths; open their eyes and ears; spend day in different directions, seeking world around or in 'em, returning to one another in the evening, ventilated, ventilating. Provision for changes in schedule. CXLVII. She brought him food. Clairvoyant, he knew it was poisonous. Third time she offered him deadly food, he accepted it, but himself appointed the hour of his death. *Religious tract David Tudor gave me : "Christ International." Train is made up of engine, coal car, caboose. Engine is fact. Coal car's faith. Caboose is feeling. Train can run with or without feeling. Caboose can't make train run.* After breakfast he offered her a cigarette. She said, "No thank you." He said, "What's wrong? Have you stopped smoking?" She said, "Yes." Next day he stopped too. That was Nobby and Beth ten years ago. CXLVIII. I've learned to say No to those I don't know. Learned to say No *to* some of those I know. (Example of underdevelopment of religious spirit.) Edwin Schlossberg and Buckminster Fuller gave six weeks comprehensive design science course at the New York Studio school. (I was invited to the last meeting. There were about twenty-two students. The first thing Bucky said was that the young people sitting around the table had sufficient intelligence to run the world, to solve all of world problems. Glancing at the students, I was skeptical. They looked like a bunch of hippies with some older oddballs thrown in.) CXLIX. (BUT WHILE THEY SPOKE, DID AS I DO AT THE MOVIES WHEN IT'S CLEAR EVERYTHING'LL TURN OUT ALL RIGHT. I WEPT. FULLER WOULD'VE SAID, "YOU SLEEP TOO MUCH.") All God's religions and all His servants (Lawmakers, Philosopher-Kings, Saints, Artists) have not been able to put Mankind back together again. "You can lead a horse to water but you can't make him drink." We've got the automobile. *No sense in leading horses around. Let'em* go where they will. Fix it so if they're thirsty there's something for'em to drink. Earth's the Way to Heaven. There's no mystery about it. Don't change Man (Fuller) : change his environment. Humanities? Save them for your spare time. Concentrate on the Utilities. *CL. In anything experienced nowadays, there is much that is true, much that is false.* Proofreading. Chadwick described magnetic effect of moon on tides, on germination of seeds. "Moon inclining draws mushrooms out of Earth." We talked of current

disturbance of ecology, agreed man's
works no matter how great are pygmy
compared with those of nature.
Nature, pressed, will respond with
grand and shocking adjustment of
creation. **Out of ourselves with a
little o, into ourselves with big O.**
**Reunion. Received month's check. Paid
bills. Went to Farmer's Market
(economy). Returned at six having
spent last penny on turkey and all
the trimmings. Friends arrived at
midnight for Thanksgiving in the Spring.
Cared for us, day in, day out, rest
of the month.**

Diary: How to Improve the World (You Will Only Make Matters Worse) Continued 1970–71

CLI. Tunnel workmen including toll-collectors went on strike. The public was put on the honor system. Once the strike was settled, receipts were examined to see how much the public had cheated the government. However, more money had been received than had been due; drivers not having change had apparently been generous. In addition the government saved all public money it would have paid its employees. We're changing from looking at the past through the rear-window to surveying it as we fly above. We see geogram of past actions plus future's wilderness. Roads that might have met didn't. They served **private ends producing impasse. Garbage behind trees is now out in the open. Anyone can see where it is.**

CLII. "REMOVE GOD FROM THE WORLD OF IDEAS. REMOVE GOVERNMENT, POLITICS from society. Keep sex, humor, utilities. Let private property go." **We also have no need for employment. We are busy doing our own work. TV. Frost interviewing Noel Coward and Margaret Mead. Sir Noel's view of life is Sir Noel. Mead's mind is large and open, like Buckminster Fuller's. She found thoughts dull that suggest that men are superior to animals or plants. Creation's and societies' differences engage her attention. They suggest the next things useful** *to be done. Vietnamese food depends on fresh* *coriander. First time I tried to find it in Chinatown, they were out of it. Second time I wasn't alone. We bought two packages : mine, from the first store, had yellowing leaves; hers, from the second, was green, luxuriant. While admiring coriander in a third store's window, she insisted we exchange packages.* **CLIII. The telephone is out of order. We're within reach of what to do by means of information. Information is what happens to us. That is, future happens before we experience it. When I was in the sixth grade, I signed up for the Glee Club. They said they'd test my voice. After doing that,** they told me I didn't have one. **Now there're more and more of us, we find one another more'n'more** *interesting. We're* amazed, when there're so many **of us, that each one is unique, different from all the others.** *Buckminster Fuller's Pollution Exploitation Corporation. Manufacturers and utilities polluting air and water do so at discrete points : smoke-stacks, open pipes, etc.* **They make the collecting of large amounts of various materials easy as pie. Once these materials are transported to the several points where they're in** DEMAND, DIRECTORS OF THE POLLUTION EXPLOITATION CORPORATION WILL SWIFTLY BECOME VERY RICH. CLIV. ASKED **what he thought of first lecture.**

Suzuki said, "Excellent, but in Zen most important thing's life." Asked next day what he thought of second lecture, Suzuki said, 'Excellent, but in Zen most important thing's death." "How can you say life one day and death the next?" "In Zen there's not much difference between the two." Lois Long received a commission to make a design to be printed on toilet paper. Unstimulated by the notion of making floral designs, she asked me if I had any ideas. Dollar bills. *Meals without beans are unbeneficial.* Telephone Company should have its system examined. Not even oriental philosophy. Just electroanalysis. *CLV. He was driving a taxi in Miami to make* enough money to sit cross-legged in Japan. *(Invitations received. We're going to the party.)* California fishermen're quarrelling with fishermen from Equador over the right to fish for poisoned fish. An American lady living in Paris maintained a bank-account in her home-town, Buttonhole, Ohio. Finding it difficult to keep accounts straight, she frequently wrote to the bank asking for extension of credit, concluding each letter : "Love, Mrs. So-and-So." Once, her circumstances seeming perilous, she telegraphed. Bank replied : "Dear Mrs. So-and-So. Don't worry. Love, Bank." We're cheered by Berkeley, Amsterdam

(fact their city councils include revolutionary leaders). Nevertheless, we know the best government's no government at all. We bow, not with a sense of duty, just to save our skins. We renounce privileges of democracy. We dream of the day when no one knows who's President, because no one bothered to vote. CLVI. Hitchhiker told me all you have to do now, no matter what city you're in, is go to that part of town where people are friendly. "You don't even have to have met them BEFORE; THEY'RE SURE TO GIVE YOU A **place to sleep, something to eat. Brotherhood."** *Each one of us was born by means of an I Ching-like chance operation (DNA-RNA; number 64, trigrams, hexagrams.) If life were not that haphazard, two adults reproducing more than once would always have the same child .* Programmed music. Why is it that children, taught the names of the months and the fact that there are twelve of them, don't ask why the ninth is called the seventh (September), the tenth called the eighth (October), the eleventh called the ninth (November), the twelfth called the tenth (December)? CLVII. I was so excited when I drove to the S&H redemption center in Flushing that I forgot to put a dime in the parking meter. When I came out with the blender and the electric blanket I had a twenty-five dollar ticket on the windshield. Sang backstage so no one could see who it was singing. "Who sang that song?" What do you want to know for? "I want to use that voice in my next opera." **Most people over thirty-five're technologically immature.** **World patriotism.** Ancient Chinese **was free of syntax. Words floated in no-mind space. With the passing of centuries, fixed relations between words became increasingly established. The history of Chinese language resembles that of a human body that, aging, becomes arthritic. CLVIII. Only chance to make the world a success for humanity lies in technology, grand possibility technology provides to do more with less, and indiscriminately for everyone. Return to nature as nature pre-technologically was, attractive and possible as it still in some places is, can only work for some of us.** After Dad died, Mother noticed I was filling out an application for increasing her Social Security. She said, "There's something you don't know." I said, "Aunt Marge told me : you were married before marrying Dad." Mother said, "That's not all. I was married three times." "What was your first husband's name?" Mother said, "You know? I've tried but I've never been able to remember." CLIX. There are *two kinds of music that interest me now. One is music I* *can perform alone. Other's music that everyone (audience too) performs together.* *Finnegans Wake* **employs syntax.** *Though Joyce's subjects, verbs and objects are generally unconventional, their relationships are the ordinary ones. Exception : the Ten Thunderclaps. Speaking without syntax, we notice that cadence, Dublinese or ministerial, takes over. (Looking out the rear-window.) Therefore we tried whispering. Encouraged, we began to chant. (The singer was sick.)* **If a diabetic uses large amounts of Vitamin C, it makes it difficult for a doctor to analyze his urine. If you have gall stones and take Vitamin C, you get worse and the gall stones get better. Otherwise, Vitamin C is as close to a panacea as the human race has managed to get.** CLX. Vitamin C's one fault is that it's cheaper and more popular than highly advertised, often dangerous, drugs. Therefore, the American medical-industrial combine warns the public : Vitamin C can be hazardous to your health. What they mean is : We want more of your money. *Asked what changes in Twentieth Century struck her as being most remarkable, Margaret Mead mentioned TV (possibility of seeing what's happening before historians touch it up).* "*Your* thinking's full of holes." That's the way I make it. **While attending an afternoon**

garden-party in Paris, a French Countess suffered an attack of diarrhea. She was wearing a georgette dress and large wide-brimmed hat. After some time, feeling a certain sense of recovery, she decided to go home. No sooner was she in the street than she felt her diarrhea returning. CLXI. Copper essential to efficiency in our domestic telephone system was removed in order to establish a Vietnamese **telephone system that'd really work.** *Margaret Mead mentioned hair : whether it grows shoulder-length or longer as with Caucasians, up and out as with Blacks, it has proved a source of profound irritation to the old generation. She said old people can't know what* **being young now is like and that young people can learn nothing from the old. If something won't return to nature, return it to itself, or use it for something otherwise useless, art for** instance. **Looking for some place to go, she noticed a Metro-station. She rushed downstairs to the ticket-office and asked the man there where the nearest WC was. He said : We don't have one. She said : Come now, my dear man, you must have something. Absolutely anything will do.** CLXII. *Fact I was depressed depressed him.* **We don't fear anarchy : we fear government.** *Neti-Neti* : "This is an extremely difficult thing to do, because it is no more an automatic activity but depends on the strength of our purpose to drop what has been the framework of our lives, and see everything afresh." *The tin and tungsten that we're in* Vietnam to get are resources we no **longer need. While our backs were turned, technology changed. U.S.A. has nothing to fight for. We are in Vietnam for no good reason.** *English doctor, asked what he thought commonest human condition was, said, "Deficient drainage."* CLXIII. Melody. *He said : Well, as a matter of fact, we do have a place, but it doesn't seem appropriate, considering the way you're dressed. She said : Lead me to it. He took her through the gate and half-way down the subway platform opened a door which he closed after she entered. Fuller says words "up" and "down" are non-descriptive of our space existence. We go, he says, out from or into the earth. Student, worried about man's accelerated alteration of his environment, asked where he should look when nature's eliminated (so to speak). Fuller said, "Look up!" He could have said : Look out! Or, even : Look in!* **CLXIV. The motel room had ten chairs, one of them straight-backed, two television sets, one non-functioning, two baths, one without hot water. View from the windows was of the windows in the next building.** let Me hAve youR

baggage; i will Carry it for you. no
nEed : i'm wearing aLl of it. **Sometimes
we blur the distinction between art and
life; sometimes we try to clarify it. We
don't stand on one leg. We stand on both.
Lady in the Telephone Company
explained why friends, after dialing my
number, sometimes get me, sometimes get
someone else. She said, "If someone
calls you while the circuit's overloaded,
we give 'em the next number. If your
last digit's 3, we give 'em 4. If
circuit's still overloaded we give 'em 5,
etc. If, after ten successive
attempts, circuit's still overloaded, we
give 'em busy signal."** CLXV. As
population goes up, average age of
people living goes down. **Teen-agers
become the majority. Students of
the World, Unite! The revolution will
be simple, like rolling off a log.** THE
OUTSIDE WALLS OF BUILDINGS IN PARIS ARE
USED FOR TRANSMITTING IDEAS. RUE DE
VAUGIRARD, I READ : LA CULTURE EST
L'INVERSION DE L'HUMANITÉ. The room
was very small. The brim of her hat
**touched its four walls. There was only a
drain in the floor with two
platforms for her feet. An automatic
flushing periodically flooded the
room. The Metro employee returned to his
ticket-office.** *To raise language's
temperature we not* only remove syntax : we
give each letter undivided attention,
setting it in unique face and size;

to read becomes the verb to sing.

CLXVI. **Day after we arrived in Los Angeles,** the police killed **one** teen-ager and wounded nine others. Whereas getting wrong numbers used to produce irritation among telephone subscribers, it now brings about a sense of community and **amusement among people otherwise unacquainted.** **The New York Telephone Company is systematically multiplying by ten the number of each subscriber's friends.** **That night, while closing up, he recalled he had not noticed the lady returning through the gate.** **He decided to check whether or not she was still in the station.** **As he came down the platform toward the WC, he heard loud beating on the door and her shouts from within.**

CLXVII. *Once France got out of Vietnam, Paris filled up with excellent Vietnamese restaurants.* **Vietnamese food should be made generally available in New York and Washington.** **Though less pleasant efforts have failed, a few good meals might end the war.** *A new society exists with its own supplies and demands.* *A musician now makes his way in the world without waiting* to be fifty years old. Not so long ago, sources of money were so thoroughly cut off that most gifted musicians gave up before they were thirty just in order to eat. **After he opened the door, she furiously complained that he had** locked her in. Denying this and wishing to demonstrate how she herself might have opened the door from the inside, he took her back with him into the closet and closed the door. CLXVIII. Been robbed so often he's losing his sense of property. All efforts of the two of them failed. The door remained shut. They spent the night together. The room was flushed every few minutes. The Countess's dress was drenched. The workman's face became seriously irritated by the brim **of the Countess's hat which remained on. Her diarrhea continued.** Lots of mimeographed material's placed everyday in the faculty mail slots at the School of Music. Manuscript exhibitions are held in the hall outside. The largest exhibition in history was given by one of the instructors. Instead of throwing his year's mail away unread as the other faculty members had, he had saved every scrap. CLXIX. "We'll be remembered as those who lived in the age of Buckminster Fuller." After Fuller's third lecture at Town Hall, capacity audience gave him standing ovation. Commenting on this, Fuller said, "It wasn't for me; I'm only an average man. It was for what I'd been saying : the fact it's possible to make life a success for everyone." In and out. We're taking first steps. Soon we'll be able to walk. Preach.

We practice what we practice. As we
were walking along, she smiled and
said, "You're never bored, are you."
(Boredom dropped when we dropped our
interest in climaxes. Socrates. Even
at midnight we can tell the difference
between two Chinamen. Grey's
differentiated. Johns. Traffic's
never twice the same. We stay awake
and listen or we go to sleep and dream.)
CLXX. It used to be beautiful. Was
like a park. Now it's like a parking lot.
Another wealthy American woman living
in Paris gave a dinner party. For the
entertainment of her guests she had
engaged a string quartet. After their
performance, she gave the first
violinist an envelope, saying, "Here's
something that may enable you to
enlarge your little orchestra." Satie:
"We must be uncompromising to the end."
Do nothing for one reason only. Think
it with respect to a large number of
other reasons, preferably reasons
that're seemingly contradictory. After
hearing the end of the story, he said,
"That doesn't seem to be the end." Of
course, he's right. The story goes on
and on. CLXXI. The young are
technologically grown-up. (Music's
definitely improving. You can tell it
from the fact that more and more you
hear it in places where you can move
around. You don't sit in rows facing the
stage. It's no longer disturbing to

yourself or others if during the performance you get up and leave.) Edwin Schlossberg told me that while Fuller was writing a dedication in his book *Utopia or Oblivion*, he paused and said, "Those are not the only possibilities." American government. Its head is in the clouds : it takes the government of other countries more seriously than it does its own. CLXXII. We no longer have servants. We have hostesses. The black one is even more charming than the white one. *She said she couldn't take a large, comprehensive view of life* because of the painfulness of immediate events in the lives of her children. She needs to become blind in order to see through and beyond. (Necessary pain.) Technoanarchism (Kostelanetz). After the operation, she complained of a new and unusual ache. Doctor said : It must be in your head. However, X-rays showed he had forgotten to take his scissors out when he sewed her up. The reason we like black people isn't because they're black. We like them because they're not as grey as we are. CLXXIII. Picnic preparation in hotel room. Chicken, marinated in lemon and sake, wrapped'n'foil, left overnight, next day dipped in sesame oil and charcoal-broiled. Broccoli, sliced, was put with ginger in twenty-five packages; corn, still in husks, silk removed, buttered'n'wrapped. Noticing bathtub was full of salad, he said, "I don't want any hairs in my food." **When can we get together? "It's hard to say : I'm going** *out of town tomorrow and I'll be back sometime today."* Stopped at a gas station around noon, the second week of May, in a part of Ohio I had heard was excellent for finding morels. I asked the attendant if he would direct me to a woods where I could hunt. Looking at his wrist watch, he said, "It's too late." **CLXXIV. "Do you have a good heart?" I enjoy doing what I do. And I'm glad to be with you.** *Fame has advantages. Anything you do gets used. Society places no obstacles. Also you become of some help to those who aren't famous yet. Activity.* "What's your favorite color?" I didn't answer. "What's your favorite combination of colors?" Didn't answer. When he was in Art School, he told me, no one liked orange and red together. Then a teacher came to the school who loved orange and red together. All the students changed their minds. They discovered that they all loved orange and red together. CLXXV. *Times* published a news release from the Food and **Drug Administration listing marketed drugs that were hazardous or ineffectual. There was then an unexpected run on the market. Customers apparently feared that their**

favorite remedies would become unavailable. Settling down for the night, Thoreau's Indian guide said, "There are snakes here." Thoreau said, **"Snakes don't bother me." Indian said they didn't bother him either.** Debug world program for any kind'o'living. (We are in our technological infancy. [Tesla, who discovered alternating current, did so in this century.] Technological errors made by government, industry [DDT, ABM, SST, CIA, etc.] are those of children, who, even though they don't know what the score is, go on playing pre-technological games of POWER AND PROFIT.) CLXXVI. *Our Spring Will Come.* **That was the title of Pearl Primus's dance for which I wrote music in the forties. It will —of course Spring will come. But before it does no amount of good weather keeps us from thinking we're in for a few more storms. We no longer need to dig in the earth for mercury. We have it in our oceans. "All we have to do is collect it when it's washed** up on **the beaches" : Edwin Schlossberg.** Susan spent three years in Europe, then was obliged to return to the U.S. She told me she was surprised to find things were going on more or less as usual. She had expected to find herself in the midst of violence, destruction, **revolution.** CLXXVII. Church was bombed.

Façade remains. Two men came to an intersection. One was blind and accompanied by his seeing-eye dog. While they waited for the light to change, dog pissed on his master's leg. Blind man then fed dog some beef. Other man said : "Why reward 'im?" (Pissed on your leg.) "I'm not rewarding 'im. I'm finding out where his head is so I can kick him in the ass." *Paper should be edible, nutritious. Inks used for printing or writing should have delicious flavors. Magazines or newspapers read at* **breakfast should be eaten for lunch. Instead of throwing one's mail in the waste-basket, it** should be saved *for the dinner guests.* **CLXXVIII. Young man came to my office in the university. I asked, "What class are you in?" He said he wasn't in any class. He studied whatever he wanted to without being enrolled. That way he'd gone to several universities, leaving each when there was no further class he found useful to attend. He said, "I'm about to graduate from this place."** Nanette Hassell's dream : The adopted children wore hats that made them look like mushrooms. One of them explained why they were all so hungry : "Sometimes when he's working he forgets to feed us." **Pittsburgh steel companies now know how to keep from polluting air and water. But it'd cost too much money, they say; they say they** wouldn't have any left to pay employees. When they see how rich Fuller's Pollution Exploitation Corporation gets, they'll change their minds and claim that, after all, all that stuff is really theirs.

Diary: How to Improve the World (You Will Only Make Matters Worse) Continued 1971–72

CLXXIX. Edwin Schlossberg: "Raising animals so people will have daily protein intake doesn't make sense; think of all the land that's necessary for pasture." Solution of world food problem will involve sources of protein that stay in position, terrarium-like places, Fuller domes, self-supporting, weather-controlled environments: organic reproduction of plant foods. *Education and Ecstacy* **(George Leonard). It would be better to have no school at all than the schools we now have. Encouraged, instead of frightened, children could learn several languages before reaching age of four, at that age engaging in the invention of their own languages. Play'd be play instead of being, as now, release of repressed anger.** CLXXX. On the plane I sat next to a psychologist employed at the Galesburg mental hospital. I said I was glad students had succeeded in changing the institution. He *said, "What are you talking about?" I said, I understand patients leave the hospital and enter enliveningly into community life. He said, "That isn't true."* Use the same opening until you know all its pitfalls. *Walking toward Greenwich and Bank Streets, I noticed an open manhole with temporary toolshed. Con Edison was at work. Two tall, heavyset workmen, facing one another in the shed, were concentrating on* *something placed between them. It looked as though they were playing chess. I walked past, stopped, went back, came close to them. They were playing chess.* *CLXXXI. She'd spent two weeks in southwest Colorado working on Soleri's building that'll house three thousand people. All apartments are cubes and identical. Those that're finished are used by the workers. "If you think about it," she said, "it's awful, but if you live in it you find it's delightful."* *Mushrooms.* Teaching-machines. Therapy-machines aiding people to form their brain waves, shifting waves' shape from that of anxiety **to that of poise, invention.** He said he'd rather have half a pint of the wild ones than a gallon of the tame (speaking of wild strawberries). **Sam Moon, poet, met me at the Galesburg airport. Asked him whether he'd heard of changes in the mental hospital brought about by students. He hadn't. Doris Moon told me hospital uses dope. Doped up madmen, formerly given jobs as salesmen, seemed listless, not really interested in what they were doing. Their eyes were strange. Galesburg** *customers demanded doctors stop letting their patients out.* **CLXXXII. "Soil is as precious as pearls and water as precious as oil." (A slogan coined by the Valley of Stones Brigade of Yueh Kechuang Commune.) In 1959 we developed the program of**

"splitting the mountain, creating the soil"
so as to alter its face into fertile land.
Doesn't matter whether you're in first
class or coach. You see the same
movie. Many people are allergic to
the commercial mushroom. Donald M. Simons
tells of an acquaintance who suffers
vomiting, diarrhea and loss of
consciousness from eating any restaurant
sauce that has even a trace of a
mushroom in it. Moved to the country
for city reasons : to start summer
theater; to set up electronic music
studio. Instead took to walking in
the woods. CLXXXIII. Just after ten
o'clock I cashed a check for one hundred
dollars. At noon I lost my billfold. I
spent the afternoon cancelling credit
cards. I also called the police. I tried
to remember what there was in my wallet
besides passport, bankbook, vaccination
certificate, and social security card. At
five o'clock I began drinking. (I was
invited to speak to staff-members of a
Connecticut asylum. After leaving the
reception room, I walked down the hall
among the madmen toward the room where I
was to speak. When I got there I knew
what had to be said. "You're sitting," I
told the doctors, "on top of a gold
mine : share your wealth with the
rest of us!") CLXXXIV. Left college
end of sophomore year. Refused honorary
degrees. Reinforcement, positive or
negative, is besides the point. I'd been
smoking like a furnace for nearly a

week. As I was leaving, university secretary said, "You've given us a breath of fresh air." **Mao : Our point of departure is to serve the people whole-heartedly, to proceed in all cases from the interests of the people and not from one's self-interest or from the interests of a small group.** **Subjected university library to chance operations. Eighty students read four hundred books. Class becomes people. Conversation.** At nine o'clock in the evening, the phone rang. Man's voice : "Did you lose anything today?" I lost my billfold! "How much did you have in it?" Aroun' $100. "Exactly $98." Where can we meet? "Tomorrow morning at ten-fifteen at your bank." Which bank? "You know which bank. If someone there can identify you, I'll give you back your billfold." I went to sleep. *CLXXXV. Use what you have (no garbage). Beet tops with yogurt.* GALESBURG. PEOPLE STILL APPLAUDING OUR PERFORMANCE. MAN, BESIDE HIMSELF WITH ANGER, RUSHED UP. SHOUTING, HE ACCUSED OUR COMPANY OF FRAUD, ME OF DISHONORING SCHOENBERG'S NAME. I SPOKE. **He became more furious. I was silent but disturbed. Madness I'd hoped for I didn't know how to enjoy. Future made clear.** I got to the bank early. The manager said he'd *identify me*. Sam Moon gave me student proposal for changes in Galesburg hospital. He said, "It's not what you have in mind; it's a

Skinnerian nightmare." **(Teen-ager imagines that by spending time in a building marked Music he'll become a musician. Even books on the subject are apt to be confusing. I didn't learn anything to speak of about mushrooms until I met Guy Nearing.)** *CLXXXVI.* *(Mao : Everyone knows that, in doing a thing, if one does not understand its circumstances, its characteristics and its relations to other things, then one cannot know how to do it, and cannot do it well.)* *If I can't take* **what happens, I'm not** ready for **anything.** *Deinstitutionalization.* **Opium dens in China no longer exist. How did Chinese shake the habit?** *Marcel Duchamp gave me a copy of his book on King and Pawn endings. I asked him to write something in it. He wrote in French : Dear John look out : yet another poisonous mushroom Marcel* Horicon Marsh, Wisconsin, October Seventy-one. One hundred thousand Canadian geese. Highway 49 bisects marsh's northern section. Bird watchers park along the road, get out and use binoculars. Traffic including trucks continues, but geese seem undisturbed. Helicopter passing over alarmed them. As they flew up from pools and fields, sky turned black. Traffic and helicopter were no longer to be heard : Goose sounds. *CLXXXVII.* *Edwin Schlossberg : Gather information without bias. Define problems. Include* their ramifications. Find solutions using energy sources going with nature, not against nature (sun, wind, tides, not fossil fuels). Initiate action alone and with others without waiting to be told what to do. *I waited. 10:15; 10:30; 10:45. I asked the bank manager whether the branch office's address was on my bankbook. He assured me that it was.* **Revolution in China implemented in part by Big Character Posters. People, walking in the streets, receive instructions. In industrialized West, people sit at home** *glued to the TV, or drive around listening to car radios. Instead of commercials, broadcast suggestions for useful activity on the part of every man, woman, and child. Repeat every fifteen minutes.* **CLXXXVIII. Schlossberg : Fear produces non-comprehensive design science. Commoner's proposal to send sewage to the land via pipeline system is an example. What's needed are toilets automatically productive of properly treated and packaged** *dry* **fertilizers.** Motel included miserable Chinese restaurant. Restaurant had a liquor license. Down the road was The Villa. Its wine was undrinkable. Seventeen inches of snow fell. Winds rose. Traffic outlawed (state of emergency). Villa closed. Only restaurant open was Chinese restaurant. Met in the bar, got plastered. Went to dining room; food was delicious. Poster in River Falls,

Wisconsin : Ralph Nader has called upon students to organize research groups to work in the public interest . . . Corporate Responsibility; Environmental Preservation; Consumer Protection; Sex & Race Discrimination (they must mean Sex and Race *Liberation*); Support WISPIRG Wisconsin Public Interest Research Group); Student Funded and controlled. Sign Petition Today! CLXXXIX. Ten to eleven, a slight, elderly man entered the bank. The lapels of his coat were faced with fur. We shook hands. The bank manager said : It's good there're still people like you living. The man replied, "I believe in God. I think that doing as I do *people prove that God exists."* Huge 747 practically empty. Boarding pass lacked seat-assignment. Hostess dropped plan to send me back to the counter to get one. I'd said : There's plenty of room, don't you think? *We're not concerned with the audience : we're concerned with* people. "In what does the old ideology of the exploiting classes lie? It lies essentially in self-interest—the natural soil for the growing of capitalism. That is why, in the course of revolution," Mao tells us, "we must fight self." That's why the Golden Rule (Do unto others as you would be done by) turned green in the U.S.A. It took self-interest for granted. Devalue it. CXC. Student-proposed change in

Galesburg asylum was isolation of patients, separation of mad from mad, twenty-four-hour intensive supervision of each individual. *Infirmities of old age.* Now that we have everything we need, we discover that there is almost nothing that we have that we want. Rush hour : no rush. Trucks, buses, cars (Sheridan Square **NYC), complete stop. Forty-five minutes. Now and then someone moved an inch or two. Details changed. Congestion continued. Black truck driver studied situation, found a solution, cheerfully gave directions. People clapped their hands, blew their horns.** *Early morning (yesterday, melting snow) : sound of footsteps; night lights still on.*

CXCI. Bank manager insisted that identifying me wasn't necessary : I was one of the bank's depositors. The man handed me my billfold and asked me to look through it carefully and notice that nothing had been removed. First, master the endgame, then the middle and finally the opening. Thus you'll be able from the beginning to see through to the end. Mushrooms tested by feeding them to dog. After dinner, maid said : Dog's dead. Guests'n'hosts had stomachs pumped. Dog had been run over by a car. *Deschool society (Ivan D. Illich),* Education Automation *(R. Buckminster Fuller). Just as, in Buddhism, denial of cause and effect arose from the realization that* *everything's caused by everything else, so Illich's society without school isn't different from Fuller's society with nothing but* **school.** **Illich and Fuller : All there is to** do is live and learn. **CXCII. "A little child shall lead them." Edwin Schlossberg's Brooklyn Children's Museum. Eddie insisted Board of Directors include children. When Schlossberg visited Fuller, Bucky said, "Listen carefully to the children's words. I want to know each word they say."** County in Florida. Law was passed prohibiting the sale of detergents. Housewives travelled to **other counties to purchase their detergents. "We know we're breaking the law but we want to get our clothes white."** *While looking through my billfold I said, I want to share what's in it with you : $50. He didn't smile. "My work's time-consuming. This has been a serious interruption." I gave him another $20. What do you do? "I'm in Rewrite." What's that? "It's in connection with Continuity." What's your name? "So-and-So."* CXCIII. Valda said that if you change your residence every six **months you can legally free your children from compulsory education.** *I asked* Mr. So-and-So whether he had found my billfold in a taxi. He said, "I **found it in the gutter."** How old are you, dear moon? Thirteen-seven? You're still **young, are** you not? One comes, then another, and another. Who'll be held on your lap? **America's the oldest country of the twentieth century. It's made the most mistakes** of the twentieth century. Whole *Earth.* Industrialization is a self-regenerative evolutionary phenomenon which started in China at least four thousand years ago. It travelled westward, and has reached China again in vastly advanced effectiveness. (R. Buckminster **Fuller.)** *CXCIV. Ihab Hassan's book,* The Dismemberment of Orpheus, *begins with a statement by Franz Kafka : "The decisive moment in human evolution is perpetual. That is* **why the revolutionary spiritual movements that declare all former things worthless are in the right, for nothing has yet happened."** *Whole Earth Cook Book.* Our recipes are not complicated : we want to turn you on to the relaxation in simple, natural cooking. The country kitchen is a traditional gathering place. We at the Whole Earth Restaurant make a party out of preparing meals. We hope you'll do the same. (Cadwallader and Ohr.) Mao : Destruction means criticism and repudiation; it means revolution. It involves reasoning things out, which is construction. Put destruction first, and in the process you have construction. CXCV. I complimented Mr. So-and-So on the tie he was wearing. It was silk, dark red, straight and narrow; it was pinned against a pink and white striped shirt. He said, "It's a relic of a previous age." As we left the bank, there was Meg Harper, one of the Cunningham dancers. I introduced her to Mr. So-and-So and told him that the Cunningham Company was about to open in Brooklyn. I offered to arrange for him to have tickets. Mr. So-and-So said, "Thank you, but I don't want any reward." All night long, thoughts of nirvana and samsara. How exhausting! Apparently I was caught by the Buddha. (Sengai.) CXCVI. Mushrooms I found in one day were more than enough for a year. Reduce use of combustion engines. *Jim'n'Carolyn went to skyscraper Indian restaurant. Restaurant had no other customers. Food'n'view were good. Afterwards, back home, Jim noticed he didn't have his wallet.* Suzuki Daisetz : One has not understood Zen until one has forgotten it. We got rid of the wolves. Now there are too many deer. Forest ranger's proposal to reintroduce wolves was stymied by protests from profit-seeking sheepranchers. The shepherd **is a wolf** *in man's clothing.* **I haven't been to a movie for three months of Sundays. I gather from what Carolyn reports that Hollywood now produces false entertainment : unmitigated violence on the screen; snickering, laughter in the audience.** CXCVII. Jim telephoned the restaurant : Do you have my wallet? "Yes. Do you have our seat-cover." I don't know anything about your seat-cover. I just want my wallet back. "We've lost too many seat-covers and recently, also, a vase; if you'll bring us back our seat-cover we'll gladly return your wallet." THRUWAYS PROMOTE THE AUTOMOBILE INDUSTRY. PEOPLE WITHOUT **high-speed cars can't use them. They're "false utility" (Illich).** Variation : multiplying cans and bottles provides false convenience. Let each household keep its containers, taking them empty to appropriate stores to be filled. This'll bring about refreshing changes in supermarket design. Staying at home'll become as amusing as vacationing in a village in Spain. *CXCVIII. Needed new glasses. Doctor, noticing hemorrhages in my eyes, said, "Do you know you have diabetes?" Don'know. Disturbed, looked up diabetes in dictionary, decided I wasn't overly hungry, thirsty, didn't excessively urinate. Complete examination showed no diabetes. Eye-doctor said, "Well, you're just getting old. There's nothing I can do about it. I want to see you every two or three months."* **Bantam paperback anthology of the writings of Mao Tse-tung, edited by Ann Freemantle, is dedicated to Dr. Ivan D. Illich.** *Twelve disciples. One teacher. One too many.* Best things in life're free; American industry thinks we can't afford them. If we could change our language,

that's to say the way we think,
we'd probably be able to swing the
revolution. **CXCIX. On his way to**
the restaurant Jim decided that if
they refused to give him his wallet he'd
get a policeman to help him. We must
find something else to do than art :
we are going to China. We hope our visit
will leave no traces. Called Statistics
Section, Immigration Division, Canadian
Government, asked how many Americans
had recently become Canadian
citizens. They said : That takes five
years. However, in 1967, 19,038
Americans immigrated to Canada. In
1968, 20,422. In 1969, 22,785. In 1970,
24,424. U.S.A. has apparently taken
steps to solve the population
problem, but only from its own point
of view. *CC. Jack* **Collins, brilliant**
mind, spastic paraplegic, Bobby
Fischer's teacher. No one in the world of
chess is as beloved. Frequently
laughing, he gets around the apartment by
riding small tricycle. People who
don't play complain chess takes too much
time. Given the opportunity to study with
Collins, it'd be a waste of time not
to. Cherish and reuse plastic utensils and
containers. Don't throw'em away;
don't acquire more than you need. Don't
take'em with you; leave them for the next
person to use. Distinguish, as you
would in the case of mushrooms, between
those that're poisonous and those
that aren't. Do not use plastics that are

derived from fossil fuels. CCI. Midst of
these thoughts, Jim felt unusual
warmth on his back. Reaching under his
coat, he found the seat-cover stuck
to his jacket. Receiving his
wallet, his apologies were politely
interrupted. "Don't apologize : this
happens all the time." *Alternatives to
art.* Crossing bridge from Windsor, Canada,
to Detroit, Michigan, the bus driver
announced : We're now entering No Man's
Land. *A newspaperman wrote asking me to*
**send'im my philosophy in a nutshell.
Get out of whatever cage you happen to
be in. If you're a dope addict in Detroit
and happen to be hospitalized for some
reason, no problem. Someone pays you a
visit, brings you a fix, and, on the
way out, rips what he can from other
patients. CCII. Irritation in my left
eye was diagnosed by two doctors as
chalazion. "Is that a sty?" No, it's
chalazion. "Will it go away by itself?"
No, it has to be scraped out. Sue Weil
made an appointment for me in
Minneapolis four days thence which I
kept even though my eye no longer
bothered me. The doctor's office was a
museum of modern art, plus many
patients and nurses. One cheerful
nurse gave me a preliminary
examination.** **National Wildlife
Refuges : museumization of**
*wilderness. Controlled folly. Doctor
said, "Your eyes're healthy.
Nothing needs to be done." What about the*

hemorrhages? *"They're not significant. The sty will go away in six or eight months."* *What about chalazion?* *"Chalazion's a synonym for sty."* **CCIII.** **Choose among all the masters the master whose way of playing appeals to you the most.** **Then replay all of his** *games.* **Barbershop's like a community. Once you get in you don't want to leave. It's for men, women, and children. There are potted plants, flowers, two large live tortoises. Brightly colored robes to choose from.** *Antenna Enterprises.* Cry in the wilderness. We're indebted to China for its language, the I Ching, Lao-tse, Chuang-tse, Zen Buddhism too. Gunpowder we'll do without; printing'll be electronic. The Great Wall and roast pig, together with other meats, **can go. Give us the Chinese sense of nature, the Chinese sense of** society. CCIV. As we were taking off from Detroit, asked the Chinaman sitting near me whether he thought acupuncture might be used **to de-addict drug addicts. He said, "Works for arthritis and lung diseases." You think it works for drug addiction? "Perhaps it does," he said.** *Imitation of nature in her manner of operation, traditionally the artist's* **function, is now what everyone** has to do. Complicate your garden so it's surprising like uncultivated land. **Suburban policeman came to the door; he went away without making any arrests.**

If you're poor, it's illegal. If you're rich, you're automatically within the law. *What necessary mystery can many people working together make? Effective revolution. Norman Brown : What we finally seek to do is to create an environment that works so well we can run wild in it.* CCV. Fuller : I now ask cosmic questions. "Is man needed in the universe?" "Does he have a universal function?" "If he is essential what needs to be invented to improve his functioning?" "What are the largest overall trends of human evolution *that need accommodations?" Food.* Infirmities of old age (old Japanese sayings) : wrinkles on the face, dark spots grow on the skin, and the back bent; bald-headed and grey-bearded, the hands tremble, the legs totter, and gone are the teeth, hard of hearing and eyesight bedimmed; indispensable are a hood on the head, wrappers, a stick, and spectacles. **Syntax, like government, can only be obeyed. It is therefore of no use except when you have something particular to command such as : Go buy me a bunch of carrots. The mechanism of the I Ching, on the other hand is utility. Applied to letters and aggregates of letters,** it brings about a language that can be enjoyed without being understood. CCVI. then a hot-water bottle, heating stone, chamber pot, and a back-scratcher; meddlesome he is, afraid of dying, and lonesome; suspicious of others, the desire for possession grows stronger; repetitive, short-tempered and querulous; obtrusive and officious; the same stories over and over again in which his own children are *invariably praised; boastful of his health, he makes others feel tired beyond endurance.* **"It is right to rebel."** When I had a Jaguar, I noticed anyone else who drove a Jaguar. Now I'm wearing jeans instead of suits, I notice nearly everyone. **Fuller and Mao. Transform mistakes into projects, misinformation into facts. Forget yourself. Blur the distinction between Fuller and Mao. Change the environment and at the same time change man. There is no line to be drawn between the two.** CCVII. Gautham told me Indian weavers used to work alone. To increase production, assembly line methods **introduced at Ahmedabad. Workmen became unhappy. After systematic experiments, group cooperation without unhappiness was established. Five people make smallest happy group. Less than five make trouble for one another. Twelve make largest happy group; with thirteen group spirit is lost. We have learned that from here on it is success for all or** *for none. "Unity is plural and at minimum two." You and I are inherently different and complementary. Together we average as zero, that is,* as eternity. (Buckminster Fuller.) Two : one against

one. CCVIII. Mao Tse-tung : We must firmly believe that the great **majority of the masses are good and that bad elements only make up** a very small fraction. Three people are two against the other one. **Four people split into two couples, each couple intent on making** trouble for the other couple. OLD AGE OF THE U.S.A. It can't see or hear very well. It's hard for it to walk. Its face is wrinkled: its teeth're false. *Black mother'n'son in the laundromat. She was born in Barbados, went to Europe, married a doctor, became a trained nurse. Boy was born in Toronto. Jobs she takes are those permitting* her son **to accompany her. When washing machine I was using began dancing, she helped me hold it in place.**

I began this part of the diary during the Nixon administration, but did not complete it until recently. Like many other optimists I was struck dumb by the course of current events. However, now that I've managed to finish the eighth, I contemplate writing two more and have begun the ninth. A year with ten months (Oct., Nov., Dec.), each having thirty days more or less. Each day has at least one hundred words and two entries. The number of words in each entry (between one and sixty-four) is chance-determined. Sometimes a day has five or six entries. The result is a mosaic of remarks, the juxtapositions of which are free of intention.

Diary: How to Improve the World (You Will Only Make Matters Worse) Continued 1973–1982

CCIX. Englishmen drive on the wrong side
of the street : it's just as good as
the **right side.** **Mak'a slave of
yourself to poetry.** **English pronoun
I's always capitalized, no matter
where in a sentence it is.
Microbiologist (Japanese) said : Go East;
in Germany ich's never capitalized
except when it begins a sentence; in
Russia you can use I or let it go,
as** YOU CHOOSE; IN THE FAR EAST—HE MADE
A GESTURE UPWARDS WITH HIS HANDS—
WORD FOR I HAS DISAPPEARED.
Government is a tree. **Its** fruit are
people. (*Essay on Civil
Disobedience.*) As people ripen, they
drop away from the tree. (Thoreau.)
*CCX. On the boat coming over, Tibetan
monk learned to speak English very
fluently. What he did, he said, was
to take his mind and place it at the
point where in Mind the English
language is.* **Sadie Stahl, born Sadie
O'Brian, left'er money to the Church.
When Philip died, bequeathed'er fifty
thousand.** "FINER MAN THERE NEVER WAS."
SADIE MADE CERTAIN INVESTMENTS. FIFTY
BECAME TWO HUNDRED. COMPLAINED BANK
WAS TAKING ALL'ER MONEY.
MR. CUNNINGHAM SAID, "SADIE, WALK
ACROSS THE STREET. THEY'LL GIVE YOU ALL
YOU WANT." "OH! THEY WILL?" SAID
SADIE WITH A TWINKLE IN HER *eye.*
**What American industry decided about
Puerto Rico was that Puerto Rico**

would be one of its consumers. Puerto *Rico shouldn't import anything from any other country. The function of the governments (American and Puerto Rican) is to see to it that what industry wants is what happens.* **CCXI. As a New York senior citizen, I get public transportation half price except during rush hours. I can also go to movies half price if I do so in the afternoons. If I take the subway, I must buy two trips at once in opposite directions, round trip. With the bus I am free to go wherever I wish.** Western medicine continues based on error : notion that first of all pain must be relieved; that secondly erasure shall be made of whatever unusual symptoms'd arisen. That's what it is : a network of poisonous painkillers and deadly antibiotics. American doctors are steadfastly suspicious of unorthodox therapies that take the whole body into consideration, that begin with spine or with diet. **CCXII. One of the first things to be done (while there's still some energy) is to bring public signs up-to-date. Signs using language should be designed** so that they can be understood by children who don't understand that language. *Watergate. Took America two hundred years to produce its own form of theater. Cf.* **The Persians** *by Aeschylus. Noh* **drama. Boredom. Fascination. Only time I**

wrote any music was between twelve and
two when the Senators went out for lunch.
People in the audience losing their
minds. Dogs searching for bombs.
Precedents : *An American Family*; the
Warhol movies; *Happenings* in general.
If, while reading the menu, you have the
feeling that you've read it before,
best thing to do is not to order
anything. *CCXIII. He'd told his*
class to read the Bible. And so he
opened it himself. After reading a little,
he laughed, closed the book, and said,
"There's just no sense in reading it any
more." Doctor told me : at your age
anything can happen. Got rid of
arthritis by following macrobiotic
diet. Work's now taking on the aspect of
play. The older I get the more things I
find myself interested in doing. Spreading
myself thin. Schoenberg stood in front of
the class. He asked those who intended to
become professional musicians to raise
their hands. I didn't put mine up.
CCXIV. Now when we really need them, they
telephoned, while we were away, to
say they weren't coming. Carla had a
doctor's appointment for nine o'clock
in the morning. She was prompt. She
waited three hours. At noon
doctor left for lunch. Carla went
home. A few days later she received a
bill for the time she'd spent in the
waiting room. *3 teens kill 4. No*
motive! Shoes'n'clothes made in Puerto

Rico are exported to United States. What isn't sold there goes up'n'price and then goes back to Puerto Rico. There are only two **languages : one uses images and ideograms; the other uses an alphabet. In Brussels or Montreal, signs in one alphabetic language are duplicated in another. All over the world alphabetic signs should be accompanied by their equivalent in characters. We would learn Chinese just by keeping our eyes open.** CCXV. Once Suzuki said, "There seems to be a tendency towards the Good." His remark stays in my mind like a melody. What could he have meant? Heavy bread without yeast. Didn't learn how to make it until I was sixty-four. **The monks take turns : one of them reads out loud while the others are eating. They call it "the greater silence."** AMERICANS, THEIR GOVERNMENT COUPLED WITH THEIR INDUSTRY, AUTOMATICALLY BARGE IN WHEREVER THERE'S A SIGN OF CHEAP LABOR. WE'RE ALL OVER LATIN AMERICA. WE DON'T SPEAK SPANISH OR PORTUGUESE. OUR EXPLOITEES DON'T SPEAK ENGLISH. NOW THEY SPEAK WITH BOMBS HOPING SOMEDAY WE'LL UNDERSTAND. CCXVI. German pharmacist said if aspirin, instead of having been discovered long ago, had been discovered just recently, it wouldn't be possible to market it. Aspirin would not pass the present restrictions against *drugs.*

Edward Weston told me photographers photograph themselves no matter what their cameras're focused on. Using chance operations Robert Mahon's found a way to let each photograph photograph itself. **Traffic was obstructed by a medium-sized car that was standing** *in the middle of the street. It was empty except for a large gentle dog who was sitting in the driver's seat. Emily Bueno said the reason nothing'll happen in America to improve* **matters is most of the people are comfortable the way it is. (We had been talking about China and revolution.) CCXVII. The United States has turned Puerto Rico into a kind of Los Angeles, a place where there is no public transportation to speak of, nothing but private cars in greater and greater congestion. Fumes. Accidents. He told me he had waited three and a half hours for a bus.** *Received letter from journalist : put your philosophy in a nutshell. Replied : get* out of whatever cage you find yourself in. Asked to supply catchy title for conversations with Daniel Charles, suggested *For the Birds.* TV interview : if you were asked to describe yourself in three words, wha'd you say? An open cage. Satie was right : experience is a form of paralysis. *CCXVIII. Nobody voted. Government was embarrassed out of* **existence.**

Dialog. *New York's the largest Puerto Rican city in the world.* *Revision of The Golden Rule : do unto others as they would be done by.* *After Dad died, I was filling out blanks to increase Mother's Social Security. Mother noticed what I was doing. "There's something I've never told you." "I know. Aunt Marge said you were married before you married Dad." "That's not* all. I was married twice before that." "What was your first husband's name?" "Y'know? I've tried'n'tried but I simply can't remember." **Aunt Sadie. She was very elderly. She had to be put in** a home. They put her in a Catholic one. First thing Sister said was : Now Mrs. Stahl, we're going to give you a nice hot bath. Aunt Sadie brightened up. Oh! She said, haven't had one of those in a long time. *CCXIX. Replied he was a politician. I laughed : in one ear her wore an earring. He continued : "Politics is all of the actions of all of the people." The sun shines very dependably in Puerto Rico, but no steps are taken to make use of solar energy. Kudzu, introduced from Japan to control soil erosion, has overgrown American Southeast. Tubers and leaves are edible. Leaves're full of protein. Surrounded by kudzu, southerners never dream of eating it. Became millionaire in Japan :*

dehydrated kudzu leaves; marketed nutritious powder. Aunt Sadie had the Women's Club to lunch. The same day she invited the Cunninghams to dinner, Merce, his two brothers and his mother and father. When the food was served, Mr. Cunningham said, "I've never seen a chicken before with so many necks." CCXX. What is the sound that's heard when a conch shell is held to an ear? Does it originate in the shell? Or is it outside sound that went all the way in and came back out transformed? Not only is the future of music playing new experimental works in Africa'n'Third World generally, future of art lies displayed before us everywhere : the junk with which we litter both our streets and all the places in nature beautiful enough to attract us. Arriving at University of Puerto Rico were told five-month military occupation of University had just stopped. Teachers'd lectured just to collect their salaries. No students'd listened. Chancellor gave reception for us. Students'n'faculty friends we'd made didn't attend. Chancellor *didn't either. Were* told Chancellor's afraid to appear anywhere. *CCXXI. There's your Aunt Sadie walking down the street with her two fur coats on and her corset over them. She was off to church. Give her a shot of whisky, Dad said.* Taxi-driver asked whether I'd seen TV coverage of Nixon's visit to China. Said I had. "They play *The Star-Spangled Banner* better in Peking than they do here in the U.S.A." I agreed. WHAT GOOD'D IT DO IF WE GOT OUT OF PUERTO RICO? PEOPLE THERE'VE FORGOTTEN LIFE'S LIKE, WHAT FIRST THING IS EACH MORNING TO DO. WARNING ME NOT TO GO ON FOOT OUTSIDE UNIVERSITY PRECINCTS, TOLD ME SHE CARRIED A GUN JUST'N CASE. NOTICED door to her apartment had seven locks. CCXXII. To measure the duration of an experience you must know the velocity of the mind. (Ezra Pound.) Before going to Japan for a concert tour, David Tudor and **I asked for a contract. We received it. Once in Tokyo we were given another quite different contract. Asked sponsors which contract they'd follow. "Sometimes we'll follow** one and sometimes it'll be better to follow the other." **Nuclear weaponry's rational adjunct to internationalism. Each nation's married to industry. Industry's polygamous. Each nation's selfish. What's needed's intelligent equation between** *human needs and world resources. Buckminster Fuller. Read his* Critical Path. *Through electronics (Marshall McLuhan) we've extended central nervous system. International world's schizophrenic, split against itself. There's no political remedy for this disease. Power politics was its cause. Holocaust.* CCXXIII. A political structure interrupted by actions of people outside it is a political structure that's not up-to-date. Holocaust. Survivors, if any, may finally come to their senses. I remember Seattle earthquake. Neighborhood where we were living was alarmed. Left the house as others did. In vacant lot for the first time we met our neighbors. "What business have I in the woods if I am thinking of something out of the woods?" (Thoreau.) Instead of picking or buying many flowers that are all the same, get just one of a kind. Put each in its own bottle. Flower arrangement with space and the possibility of being easily changed, a mobile. CCXXIV. The day continues by becoming the night. Our dreams are closely related to our sense perceptions. Deep sleep. Then into alpha before getting up. Puerto Rico. A copy of *Newsweek* costs three fifty; *New York Times* costs two and a *quarter.* March nineteen-eighty-two. "You probably heard that we had an earthquake. Some people thought a man under the bed. Not your old Aunt Sadie. She knew." *Philadelphia : What business have I in the woods if the woods are not in me?* *Wake me up at 8:30 or 9:00, whichever* one comes first. *A way of writing which* comes from ideas, is not about them, but which produces them. CCXXV. About to leave the bus, having

gone from one town to another, told conductor no one *had collected my fare, asked him how much it was. It's free, he said. That was a few years ago in Massachusetts, in one of those three college towns that are all fairly close together.* **Now I'll go to sleep.** **In the morning ideas will come to me.** The church is not a church. **After being moved it either became an antique shop or might've.** **And then it was moved again and added on to. Church is now a living room.** *If your head's in the clouds keep your feet on the ground. If feet're on the ground, keep your head in the clouds* **CCXXVI. El Salvador.** Dreamt I'd composed a piece all notes of which were to be prepared and eaten. Lemon'n'oil, salt'n'pepper. Some raw. Finished score on day of performance. (I was to perform it.) Set out for concert hall, had difficulty finding my way. Decided to stop and rehearse. As soon as first notes were cooked, dogs and cats came around and ate them all up. Drove to the airport bumper to bumper. Back home, glued to the TV : Watergate. Ninety-six degrees : city's hydrants opened so those who wish **may cool off in the streets. Politics. We are present at the same event, but we notice** different things. CCXXVII. Adverbs, adjectives, syntax focus on perceiver rather than perceived. *Thoreau at twenty-two* *wanted to write in such a way that what he experienced could be experienced by the reader as though reader'd experienced it himself. Puns do this suddenly (Joyce, Bashō, Brown). Utility arises where it wasn't expected (even by author). Or, as in Thoreau, lucidity. Puns again : Duchamp. Lucidity again : Wittgenstein.* **At any point where a shell bulges it can be tapped like a drum; at an edge it may be plucked just as the spine of a cactus may be plucked.** The traffic never stops, night or day. Every now and then a siren. Horns, screeching brakes. Extremely interesting; always unpredictable. At first thought I couldn't sleep through it. Then found a way of transposing the sounds into images so that they entered into my dreams without waking me up. A burglar alarm that lasted several hours resembled a Brancusi.

CCXXVIII. The divorce of state'n'industry. When assigning seats for transoceanic or transcontinental flights, airline representatives will not ask whether we smoke or not nor whether we wish to sit by the window or on the aisle; they will ask what games we play. Jack Collins told me that his trip to Iceland was long and tedious. The trip back was short and pleasant : he was playing chess. **Things that might've been done that haven't yet. Electronic**

additions to plants and bushes turning them into instruments for a children's orchestra. The use of photoelectric eyes to scan the principal entrances and exits at Grand Central Station bringing about pulverization of *Muzak.*

Transformation of chorus and *orchestra into a thunderstorm. CCXXIX. Flight from Houston, Texas, to Charleston, South Carolina, took more than twelve hours. Changed planes in Atlanta. Landing in Charleston, surprised to notice mountains. Once in the airport, asked porter whether airport was newly constructed. "Only airport we've ever had." Turned out to be West Virginia. Correction flight (Charleston to Charleston) was paid for by another airline that had nothing to do with mistake.* **Aunt Sadie wasn't quite in front of the meat market that was in the building she owned. She was trying to see what was going on without being** observed. Look, she said, they're *giving* away the *nicest* bits of meat. **CCXXX. Used to smoke at least three packs a day. Everything that happened was a signal to light a cigarette. Finally I divided myself into two people : one who knew we'd stopped; the other who didn't. Everytime the one who didn't know picked up a cigarette to light it, the other one laughed until he put it down.** *In Japanese brain vowels're processed on one side, consonants on the* *other. Westerners process vowels and consonants on the same side, leaving other without any relation to language. Out of twenty-three Japanese* brains, four'r five work way Western ones do. Trust a few of us use our heads the way Japanese use theirs. **CCXXXI. Towed away in New York City. Police wouldn't accept seventy-five dollar check because I didn't own the car. Went to sleep. Dreamt I was caught speeding a week later in California. Cop said they charged fifty dollars for each person in the car. Had two friends with me. When I woke up, realized I'd saved** seventy-five dollars just *by being* **asleep.** **Enjoyed riding four-wheeled. Away from the roads and signs.** **In'er nineties,** Mrs. Dennison's very well. Except, she says, I don't have the energy **I had when I was in my seventies.** *People'n Puerto Rico who still have jobs don't have them for five days a week, just for four. Naturally they don't get as much pay as they used to, though their living expenses have skyrocketed. Those who work in hospitals stay at home for half a week. Patients get along by themselves.* **CCXXXII. Staple diet in Brazil's always been rice'n'beans. Black beans. American advisors said soy-beans would make more money. For a while that happened. Then price paid for soybeans'n Chicago slumped.**

Brazilians now standing in line to buy black beans imported at outlandish prices. Mushroom is close. Pine tree continues hiding **it with its needles.** Out of unemployment comes self-employment. There's no longer time to correct things first here and then there, say'n Puerto Rico today, South Africa tomorrow, later'n Israel or Salvador. Whole thing's wrong. Beginning of future if there is to be one is making world a single place, freeing it from its division into nations. **CCXXXIII. With the innermost part of the shell cut off, shell is trumpet, air in one** *way, out the other. But nothing's lost : sounds have been gained : leading tone to tone shell gave before being altered. The tonic's heard again by closing off cut-off end with a finger, placing shell to ear. Situation has both changed and remained* what it was. **Breakfast in Dutch hotel : tables piled high with cold bread, cold meats, cheese, cold soft-boiled eggs and butter; plastic utensils, yellow-green and orange. Guests serve themselves. Waiters are busy pouring coffee and tea, piling up used utensils, and throwing leftover food into large orange plastic garbage containers placed in the center of the dining room.** CCXXXIV. It **was a very hot summer day. Merce's mother was looking out the window. "Look, there's**

Sadie," she said, "wearing her rubbers.
No wonder her feet hurt." *If you partly
fill a conch shell with water, and
then tip the shell this way and that,
from time to time* you'll hear gurglings
over which you have virtually no control.
Contingency. People ask what the
avant-garde is and whether it's
finished. It isn't. There will
always be one. The avant-garde is
flexibility of mind and it follows like
day the night **from not falling prey to
government and education. Without
avant-garde nothing would get
invented.** *CCXXXV. I'm gradually
learning how to take care of myself. It
has taken a long time. It seems to me
that when* I **die I'll be in perfect**
condition. We've turned Puerto Rico into a
country without anything. No
fishing'r'agriculture, no industry.
Avocados'n'carrots came from Florida.
Factory-centered cities along the
southern coast're ghost towns. After
seventeen years no taxation,
profiteering companies on eighteenth
closed down or a) went bankrupt, b)
started up again under a new name.
Result : unemployment's incomplete, just
forty per cent. Concerned about her
electricity bill, Aunt Sadie switched
off anything she wasn't actually using.
She asked Merce's mother about the
refrigerator light. Mrs. Cunningham
explained it was automatic : on when the

door was open, off when it was
closed. Not convinced, Aunt Sadie
peeked. She opened the door just the
least little bit; found she was
right. "See! It's on!" CCXXXVI.
Optimism is continuous. Only the
space in which it operates expands or
contracts. Sometimes so little that
it brushes against the skin. Daniel in
the lion's den. ONE IS THEN AT HOME,
no place to go. *The night redoubles*
our energy. Imagination. **I am not a**
good historian. I don't know how many
years its been, but every now and
then, when I go out, I hesitate at the
door, wondering whether a cigarette's
still burning somewhere in the house.
The large Australian shells are as
musical **as violins.** DORIS DENNISON'S
MOTHER'S NINETY-FIVE. DORIS SAID,
"MOTHER, WHY DO YOU STILL TREAT ME
LIKE A CHILD? YOU KNOW I'M SEVENTY-FOUR."
"YOU ARE!" SAID MRS. DENNISON. "I
CAN'T BELIEVE IT."

Editors' Note

Don't know whether to read Love's Body *or out-of-date newspapers that are lying around. Everything we come across is to the point.*

—John Cage

In his introduction to *Diary: How to Improve the World (You Will Only Make Matters Worse)* 1965, John Cage describes it as "a mosaic of ideas, statements, words, and stories." He then adds (before going on to explain how he constructed the mosaic): "It is also a diary." Despite the fact that Cage appears to slightly downplay this aspect of the piece, it is a crucial factor in separating *Diary* from much of his other work. He often spoke about resisting the traditional emphasis on individual taste and the perspective of the artist in the formation of his work. Yet, *Diary* draws from and looks out to the world, containing Cage's opinions and views on innumerable subjects, through which we see his particular predilections, obsessions, and quirks. And though chance played a major role in both the assembling and the look of the material, that material accumulates into a complex reflection of Cage's own sensibilities as a thinker and citizen of the world; thus his social awareness, idealism, and sense of humor all emerge as primary qualities throughout *Diary.*

In much the same way that Samuel Pepys's diary describes life in 17th century London, Cage's *Diary* (written between 1965 and 1982) stands as a valuable time capsule and embodies the zeitgeist of a period in which there was much tumult, a belief in revolution, and an idealistic investment in the redeeming qualities of individual human beings (as opposed to the power government and big business wield). A list of all of the topics included in *Diary* is too long to include here, but even a brief sample will give the reader an idea of the enormous range of subjects which occupy Cage's thinking: politics, philosophy, war, technology, transportation, mushrooms, the fate of the environment, globalization, over-population, and the art-life continuum. Cage's family (his parents in particular) are very present as are numerous friends, colleagues and inspirations (Fuller, McLuhan, Duchamp, Ramakrishna, to name just a few). There are also references to the sometimes banal details of Cage's familial and domestic life as well as his responses to current world events.

In keeping with much of his work, disparate elements are brought together as a collage, and he used I Ching-determined chance operations for the physical characteristics of *Diary* (number of words per entry, typography, indentation, etc.). He often employed larger than usual spacing between sentences as well as the individual entries; this has the effect of blurring the lines between the end of one entry and the beginning of the next.

Cage began *Diary* in 1965, initially as a text to be published in Clark Coolidge's journal *Joglars*. A year later, Cage gave the first of several lectures using *Diary* as his text. In 1992 Wergo released a multiple CD recording of all the completed parts of *Diary* (with Cage reading the text and employing chance-determined variances in volume), but the texts were never published together; rather, they were included in three different volumes by Wesleyan University Press (Parts I – III in *A Year From Monday*, Parts IV – VII in *M*, and Part VIII in *X*). One of our primary goals in bringing together all eight sections was to make it much easier to read *Diary* all the way through and thus enable the reader to experience it as a unified work. In fact, Cage planned ten sections and was at work on the ninth part when he died: *Diary* is a work that occupied him—albeit sporadically—over the last thirty or so years of his life.

In this volume, the text and line breaks are reproduced as they were published in the Wesleyan volumes. Furthermore, we consulted typed drafts as well as hand written versions in Cage's steno notebooks which reveal more about Cage's process. For example, the "master" page covering entries CCIX-CCXXXVI reveals that Cage determined how many words would be used for each entry. As each day required one hundred words, he continued to create additional materials until the limit was reached (or exceeded slightly in order to finish a thought or sentence). Furthermore, Cage drew a circle around each number when the entry was completed and drew a square over numbers for which an alternative version was available.

Rather than reproduce *Diary* in black ink as in the Wesleyan publications, we were inspired by the use of color (as well as the greater variety of typefaces) applied to Part III, published as a Great Bear Pamphlet in 1967 by Something Else Press. Dick Higgins and Alison Knowles, in collaboration with Cage, employed a two-color process (using various

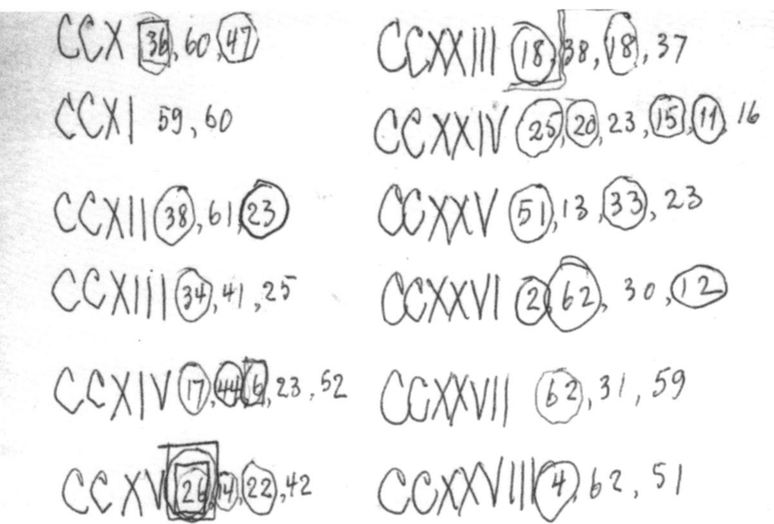

Detail of photocopy of one of John Cage's steno notebooks. Courtesy of John Cage Trust.

mixtures of red and blue) to add another chance-determined layer to the text. The use of color was an additional step which imbues the text with greater physicality, something that seems both musical and sculptural. The varying typefaces, the patterns of indentation, and most dramatically, the shifts in color give the words a spatial dimension. These qualities ask us to hear the words as well as see them.

Using the IC number generator (based on the *I Ching*) developed for Cage by Andrew Culver, we reworked all eight sections with chance operations, determining typeface, color and indentation from the left margin. We also used a set of eighteen typefaces very similar to the Great Bear pamphlet and the two original colors, with twenty-eight variations depending on the ratio of their mixture. (Our task was greatly helped by the generosity of James Hoff of Primary Information who, having re-printed the Great Bear Pamphlet in 2007, shared his files with us.) In our early conversations about the project with Laura Kuhn, director of the John Cage Trust, she stressed Cage's belief that the success of chance determinacy depends on the quality of the questions being asked. (In other words, if you ask a poor question you will get an unsatisfactory result, one that may, for example yield a loose formal structure.) After consulting Cage's introduction to part one of *Diary*, we formulated the following set of questions:

1. Is the entry a single typeface? If so, which one?

2. If not, how many words before a new typeface is introduced? And does this new typeface run to the end of the passage? (If not, repeat questions 1 and 2 until the end of the passage.)

3. How many spaces from the left margin does the line begin?

4. Is the entry a single color? If so, which one?

5. If not, how many words before a new color is introduced? And does this color run to the end of the passage? (If not, repeat questions 4 and 5 until the end of the passage.)

For those readers who may be wondering how exactly a chance operation is performed, consider the first question above. We assigned each of the two possible answers a number, then consulted the number generator. The number 1 signified that the entry should be a single typeface while the number 2 signified that the typeface should change. Given an answer of 1, we consulted the number generator to choose a typeface (each was assigned a number from 1 to 18). When the answer was number 2, we counted the number of words in the entry and asked the number generator how many words a typeface should be applied to.

We quickly discovered that what appeared to be a rather mundane procedure yielded magical results. With each question the text was transformed, becoming more musical and more sculptural with every step. Take, for example, the evolution of entry LXXVII of *Diary*:

LXXVII.   He
refuses to give up.   When he walks
across the room, you wonder whether he's
going to make it (a strange orientation of
the upper body in relation to the
legs, an original way of putting one
foot in front of the other).   Out of
Illinois into Sweden.   (How will it
happen?   Will we do it or will it be

done to us? Unemployment.) Climate
control. Stravinsky's objection to
Schoenberg's music : it isn't modern (too
much like, though more interesting than,
Brahms'). Absence of modernity's
effect of Schoenberg's accepting
tradition, hook, line and sinker.
Sounds everywhere. Our concerts
celebrate the fact concerts're no
longer necessary.

LXXVII. He
refuses to give up. When he walks
across the room, you wonder whether he's
going to make it (a strange orientation of
the upper body in relation to the
legs, an original way of putting one
foot in front of the other). *Out of
Illinois into Sweden. (How will it
happen? Will we do it or will it be
done to us? Unemployment.) Climate
control. Stravinsky's objection to
Schoenberg's music : it isn't modern (too
much like, though more interesting than,
Brahms'). Absence of* **modernity's
effect of Schoenberg's accepting
tradition, hook, line and sinker.
Sounds everywhere. Our** concerts
celebrate the fact concerts're no
longer necessary.

LXXVII. He
refuses to give up. When he walks
across the room, you wonder whether he's
going to make it (a strange orientation of
the upper body in relation to the

legs, an original way of putting one
foot in front of the other). *Out of*
Illinois into Sweden. (How will it
happen? Will we do it or will it be
done to us? Unemployment.) Climate
control. Stravinsky's objection to
Schoenberg's music : it isn't modern (too
much like, though more interesting than,
Brahms'). Absence of **modernity's**
effect of Schoenberg's accepting
tradition, hook, line and sinker.
Sounds everywhere. Our concerts
celebrate the fact concerts're no
longer necessary.

LXXVII. He
refuses to give up. When he walks
across the room, you wonder whether he's
going to make it (a strange orientation of
the upper body in relation to the
legs, an original way of putting one
foot in front of the other). *Out of*
Illinois into Sweden. (How will it
happen? Will we do it or will it be
done to us? Unemployment.) Climate
control. Stravinsky's objection to
Schoenberg's music : it isn't modern (too
much like, though more interesting than,
Brahms'). Absence of **modernity's**
effect of Schoenberg's accepting
tradition, hook, line and sinker.
Sounds everywhere. Our concerts
celebrate the fact concerts're no
longer necessary.

In addition to the wonder at seeing the text transform, the process also presented both a challenge and a lesson with regards to the imposition of personal taste. Where one's formal instincts might want things to look a specific way (the desire, perhaps, for a splash of red to break up a section that was mostly blue), chance operations require generosity and trust: to be open to the world and all its possibilities. Ultimately, if the questions have been properly framed, any and all results are good, which of course is not the same as *anything* being good.

Cage himself often spoke of the *I Ching* as a utility for the world. It's our hope that in bringing all eight parts of *Diary* together in a single volume that it might function in a similar way. For all of Cage's optimism and hope that the world could be improved, he also (as the title reveals) seemed to accept the paradox inherent in such an attempt. In its acceptance of human nature and its allowance for us to exist imperfectly while still reaching for a more perfect world, *Diary* sustains repeated readings and the possibility to discover new ways of thinking about the predicaments we face, then as now.

—Richard Kraft and Joe Biel, 2015

The Eleventh Thunderclap

John Cage's *Diary: How to Improve the World (You Will Only Make Matters Worse)* is indeed a diary, but with a difference: it presents a meandering self-observation of the unselfconscious life of the mind. It is a revelatory rendering of the flux of the social world, a monologue of poetic insight dispersed in agile anarchy over a narrative field, punctuated by the incisiveness of Zen. The constructed world of technology and the disordered simultaneity of world events both intrude and retire. Its center is everywhere and nowhere. Mushrooms and friends appear and disappear. The process never quite arrives at a full stop for *Diary* takes shape as a mindstream breaking into disjunct sidestreams of flow, always inflected with good humor, sometimes with penetrating admonition, but adhering to the guidance of chance operations and the model of nature. Cage's experimental diary reveals a portrait of the artist as public intellectual at the peak of his musical career who is also attempting to escape from demands on his time by an admiring public. His own exacting compositional regime is mirrored here in an amiable and charming piece of writing.

Diary's mordant title alludes to our current predicament, which resembles the world's predicament in 1965 when Cage began to publish this project in installments. Take it, if you will, as a manifesto for change, a book of changes. Cage's prescience concerning the complications of technology in the twenty-first century seems uncanny. A few examples will suffice: *We need for instance an utterly wireless technology*, he stated; adding: *all technology must move toward the way things were before man began changing them: identification with nature in her manner of operation, complete mystery.* Cage imagined the internet as a *universal language, a universal culture, and a universal common market.* He foresaw *instant universal voice communication ... but also instant television, instant newspapers, instant magazines and instant visual telephone service ... the development of such global communications system would link people everywhere.* Like his compadre Marshall McLuhan, the Canadian media theorist, Cage understood convergent media, as in this imagining of smartphones and eBooks: *Add video screen to telephone. Give each subscriber a thousand sheets of recordable erasable material so anytime, anywhere, anyone'd have access to a thousand sheets of something (drawings, books, music, whatever).* He even pinpointed the structural deformations of terrorism over state warfare: *War will not be group conflict: it'll be murder, pure and simple, individually conceived.* John Cage also foresaw that digital utilities mask their dystopian consequences: we become digital tourists in a state of terminal duplication.

Cage's premonitions about digital technology were embedded in his concern for the social world in an authentic search for what he styled *world improvement* or what he might have called "social revolution." However, he preferred to conjoin the positive connotation of *improvement* to the suspicion that we are blind to our lapses of making matters worse. His earliest writings evince the hopefulness of changing the mind: in a speech for Los Angeles High School in 1927 titled "Other People Think," he envisioned, at the age of sixteen, a "Science of Appreciating, Respecting, and Sympathizing with Others." Cage understood the imperative necessity of moving from an economy of scarcity to an economy of abundance. He expressed with brilliant clarity the necessity of meeting human needs in a personal letter of January 29, 1973 to Polish composer Mirek Kondracki:

> The problem nowadays is that our experience is necessarily *social*: we can no longer tolerate the division of human beings into those who have what they need to live and those who do not have what they need to live; and we can no longer tolerate our continuing actions which bring the environment close to total destruction. We are in a situation where disastrous mistakes must cease being made.

Even with this vital realization, *Diary* further reveals the perspicacity of an artist whose cogent reflections about social inequality and environmental catastrophe are interwoven into the daily fabric of his lifelong experimentalism in music and art.

Also blended into *Diary* are the interpenetrations of chance operations with quotidian trivia, of the music of Eric Satie with the civil disobedience of Thoreau, of the circularity of James Joyce's *Finnegans Wake* with the pleasure of mushroom hunting. Mycology for Cage became as indispensable an oracle as the *I Ching* in exploring possibilities for musical composition. The murmuring cosmos of the fungi concealed for him the secret of silence throughout the rhizosphere and the deep woods, and the process of encountering mushrooms helped to spark the realization that silence is ambient sound. Cage positioned mushroom hunting as a para-musical phenomenon – the perfect enterprise for appreciating silence and engaging with chance. Cage believed that he was *more alive when not knowing*, preferring the role of student over teacher, yet always potentiating the synergy between the two. His definition of education: *People together without restrictions in a situation abundantly implemented.*

If mushrooms lead to nature, and thus to silence, it was *Finnegans Wake* that provided one model of a recombinant wordscape to unspool everyday experience onto the proving ground of his experimental writing. Cage recycled the Wake in several "writings through" but complained mildly that though Joyce's subjects, verbs, and objects seem unconventional, their relationships are quite ordinary. That is, Joyce adhered throughout to syntactical structure even in the linguistic *pot pourri* of the Wake. To this observation Cage found an exception in the Wake's ten thunderwords – Joyce's periodic hundred-letter words that condense history and technology into mighty, polysemantic blasts of Language. In its totality, Cage's *Diary* can be seen to function as the eleventh thunderclap, extending the Wake's range of hyperlinked wordplay into the postmodern complexities of the 60s and 70s. He thereby tuned in to transformations of digital image and text yet to come.

In his life John Cage experienced both homelessness and international fame, and yet he always seemed brightly optimistic: *We have only one mind (the one we share).* If this salutary idea now seems threatened in the bitter divisiveness of the rise of fascism and tribal nationalism in America, then we urgently need to nurture a playful facility of mind in order to demilitarize language and reinvent the commonality that seems to slip away from us. Cage developed the principle of the interconnectedness of the shared mind in the way he selflessly championed musicians, dancers, artists, and iconoclastic thinkers. His benevolent projection of life through the chaos of politics shines resplendently in

Diary: How to Improve the World (You Will Only Make Matters Worse). In his future electronic democracy Cage envisioned a global utilities network for everyone (water, food, shelter, clothing, electricity, audio-visual communication, transportation). Yet he commended a basic recipe for improvement that was very simple: to improve society, spend time with people you haven't met, a notion he borrowed from the critic Paul Goodman. You will improve the world by reading, and then by abundantly implementing, John Cage's *Diary*. Its meaning resides in its use.

—David W. Rose, January 21, 2019

A selection of pages from the incomplete and unpublished Part IX

What might Part IX of *Diary* have included had Cage been inclined to complete it? What was missing from the previous eight? It's hard to know for sure from the single notebook left behind, but Cage shared what appear to be ready thoughts on the subject in a conversation with Klaus Schöning in 1991 (reproduced in the CD booklet to the 1992 Wergo recording of *Diary*): praise of the macrobiotic diet, which he'd been faithful to for years, but also acupuncture, Chinese herbs, and chiropractic, all of which he'd in the interim added to his health regime. Also AIDS, at the time rampant and newsworthy, and death, although he was quick to add that it's not so much one's own death that might warrant reflection but rather "the death of the people you have known for so long in your life." He adds mesostic poems to his list, a few of which grace Part VIII, and, of real topical significance, nanotechnology, or what he gleefully referred to as "technology without pollution." This had captured his imagination at the time through the writings of K. Eric Drexler: *Engines of Creation: The Coming Era of Nanotechnology* (1990) and *Unbounding the Future: The Nanotechnology Revolution* (1991). These writings led Cage naturally to the subject of robots and robotics, which he believed would be a means to "free us all from our own work."

Very little of this shows up in the scant manuscripts left behind in a single red notebook at the time of his death in 1992. Did Cage lose interest in the project, or was it that other commissions and interests simply demanded more immediate attention? We'll never know for sure.

So that the reader may have a glimpse and formulate her own questions, we include a sampling of pages (chosen solely on the basis of legibility) from the only known materials from the unfinished Part IX now held in the archives of the John Cage Trust.

—Laura Kuhn, Director of the John Cage Trust, 2019

108 SHEETS COLLEGE RULE

9½ in. x 6 in. 241 mm x 152 mm

Top Scholar®

No. 12003 TOP SCHOLAR COLUMBIA, MD. 21046

MADE IN U. S. A.

3

Robots making robots.

12

Our questions live in the world. World is a world of answers.

CCXL 8

Being alive is sufficient reason for having credit.

2

Reverent intensity.

17 The munitions industry is not on
our side nor is it on theirs;
it's on its side.

48

In a way that escaped our notice New York became beautiful. Everywhere you look. Maybe it's because the buildings aren't automatically torn down anymore. ~~People~~ We seem to be holding on to them, taking care of them. Architectural details. As much variety in a single panorama as in Rome.

15

The church bells still ring. The swallows make music before breakfast. All is not lost.

16

When d'you suppose the sun'll come out?
Maybe we've done something to
permanently damage the weather.

16

More'n' more'n New York City you see people walking around in the streets without any clothes on.

26

Bill and Elaine de Kooning were flying to Amsterdam. Shortly after the movie had started, Bill got up and said, "This's no good: let's go ~~home.~~ home."

~~outside~~

~~out."~~

24

Since they're unemployed, governments fiddle around, trying to make a wave here or there in order to have a reason for raising, or lowering, the taxes.

18

Rome at its height was a society of slaves and the rich. The rich, of course, were unemployed.

47

Seeing well-known and unknown as different sides of same coin. When Thoreau was alive and gave a talk only two or three ~~ott~~ people listened to what he had to say. Were he to give a lecture now no matter what the subject the place would be mobbed.

28

Walking up Sixth Avenue. Young fellow asked, "Know where's an open store? I'm hungry." There's a health food store down there. "Don't want health food. I want junk food."

32

Going to school not in order to
prepare for a job but just
to find out what it is that
interests ~~you~~ us, what it is
you ~~we~~ ~~you~~ want to spend ~~your~~ ~~our~~ your
~~time~~ life doing.

24

Accidentally dropped on ~~the~~ a tan wall-to-wall carpeting. Tea grounds: McGrath's Original Irish Blend. Rapidly picked up. Next morning, quite dry, orange glow suggesting Tobey monoprint.

12

All of the answers (the *I Ching*) answer all of the questions.

42

Sunday morning in Bremen. Turned on English-speaking radio hoping to hear the news. Instead was taken to church. Story from the New Testament. Jesus raised from the dead giving the men tips on how to catch fish. Tears came to my eyes.

16

This is the first of the global commandments:
Thou shalt not divide the world into
nations.

CCLXVI 10

Music ~~makes it possible to~~ gives us practice in reading things we can't understand.

Bloomingdale's. Ordered blinds. Saleslady said, "Have them myself. You'll never regret it." Months later blinds arrived. Called to say hadn't received a bill. "You'll get one. Just wait." Months later wishing not to lose ~~jeopardize~~ my ~~credit~~ standing ~~remain in good standing~~ called again. "We have problem. Can't send ~~you~~ bill. You haven't enough credit to have ordered blinds in first place." Shall I come up & write you a check? "Oh! Would you?"

12

Answer takes on different meaning for each question even the repeated question.

CCXXXVII 2, 45, 55
CCXXXVIII 34, 3, 16, 55
CCXXXIX 51, 4, 40, 12
CCXL 8, 10, 43, 2, 56
CCXLI 41, 23, 32, 17
CCXLII 55, 62
CCXLIII 55, 54
CCXLIV 29, 47, 48
CCXLV 31, 4, 2, 15, 52
CCXLVI 62, 16, 53
CCXLVII 8, 29, 56, 52
CCXLVIII 40, 7, 63
CCXLIX 7, 16, 26, 14, 27, 22
CCL 2, 19, 21, 51, 24
CCLI 35, 25, 56
CCLII 33, 18, 39, 47
CCLIII 54, 21, 58
CCLIV 54, 28, 32
CCLV 56, 50
CCLVI 62, 24, 35
CCLVII 63, 49
CCLVIII 16, 38, 41, 58
CCLIX 30, 56, 30
CCLX 40, 32, 16, 12
CCLXI 37, 63
CCLXII 44, 33, 59
CCLXIII 26, 42, 25, 43
CCLXIV 63, 35, 27
CCLXV 45, 25, 16, 2, 23
CCLXVI 10, 29, 64
CCLXVII 4, 12, 53, 29, 21